# Disney INF(IN)ITY

### INFINITE POSSIBILITIES. ENDLESS FUN.

# OFFICIAL GUIDE

BOURNEMOUTH LIBRARIES

620312424 0

PUFFIN BOOKS

Published by the Penguin Group: London, New York, Australia, Canada, India,
Ireland, New Zealand and South Africa
Penguin Books Ltd, Registered Offices: 80 Strand, London WC2R 0RL, England

puffinbooks.com

First published 2014
001

Written by Richard Jenkins
Text and illustrations copyright © Disney, 2014

© Disney. © Disney/Pixar. © Disney Enterprises, Inc. and Jerry Bruckheimer, Inc. The LONE RANGER property is owned
by and TM & © Classic Media, Inc., an Entertainment Rights group company. Used by permission. The term Omnidroid
used by permission of Lucasfilm Ltd. Slinky® Dog © Poof-Slinky. FIAT is a trademark of FIAT S.p.A. Volkswagen
trademarks, design patents and copyrights are used with the approval of the owner Volkswagen AG. Chevrolet Impala is a
trademark of General Motors. Hudson Hornet is a trademark of DaimlerChrysler Corporation. Sarge's rank insignia design
used with the approval of the U.S. Army. Cadillac Range background inspired by the Cadillac Ranch by Ant Farm (Lord,
Michels and Marquez) © 1974.

All rights reserved

Made and printed in Slovakia

Except in the United States of America, this book is sold subject to the condition that it shall not, by way of trade or
otherwise, be lent, re-sold, hired out, or otherwise circulated without the publisher's prior consent in any form of binding
or cover other than that in which it is published and without a similar condition including this
condition being imposed on the subsequent purchaser

British Library Cataloguing in Publication Data
A CIP catalogue record for this book is available from the British Library

ISBN: 978–0–14135–333–3

# INFINITE POSSIBILITIES. ENDLESS FUN.

# OFFICIAL GUIDE

# CONTENTS

# THE TOY BOX

# TOY BOX ADVENTURES

# ONLINE

# FOR FUN

# WELCOME TO

## Disney

## INFINITY

### INFINITE POSSIBILITIES. ENDLESS FUN.

**R**ead on to discover the limitless world of Disney Infinity. Along with essential guides to every Play Set and pointers on how to create mindblowing Toy Box adventures, this book will be your constant companion as you play through the Disney Infinity game. It's packed with tips, tactics and secret information you won't find anywhere else. And remember there are no rules . . . just infinite possibilities!

The more you play, the more you unlock. And the more you unlock, the more possibilities for play. Tick off the handy *Got it!* boxes as you go.

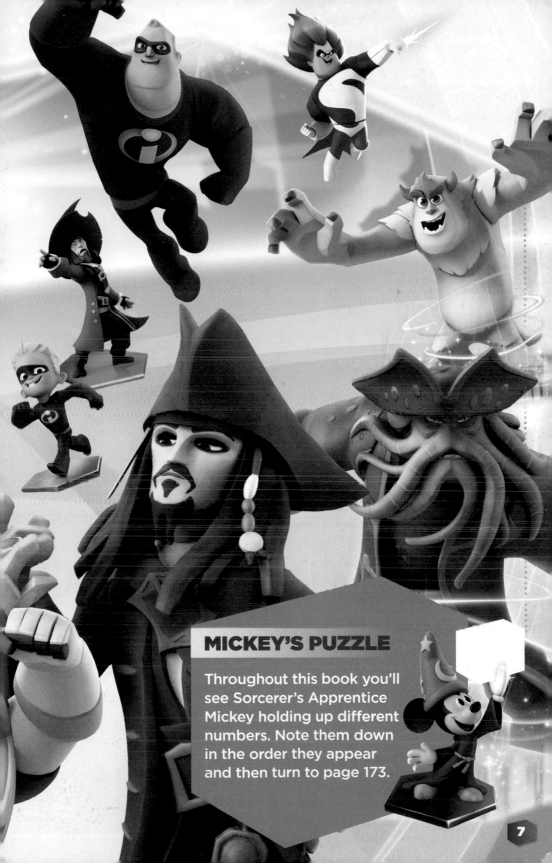

## MICKEY'S PUZZLE

Throughout this book you'll see Sorcerer's Apprentice Mickey holding up different numbers. Note them down in the order they appear and then turn to page 173.

# GETTING STARTED

**Disney Infinity comes in two amazing parts . . .**

## PLAY SET MODE

### Play in their worlds

Each Disney Infinity Play Set is like a whole new game. Place your Disney Infinity Figure and Play Set piece on to the Infinity Base to jump into a mission within that world. Take on the role of Sulley, the lovable scarer, become Captain Jack Sparrow, the sword-wielding pirate, or transform yourself into Mr. Incredible, and get ready to save Metroville from the Omnidroids!

- Incredibles
- Monsters University
- Pirates
- The Toy Box
- Options

## TOY BOX MODE
### *Infinite possibilities*

And, if that's not enough, the Toy Box opens up a whole new world. Let your imagination run wild and mash up characters, vehicles and locations to create awesome new adventures. As you journey through the different Play Sets, you'll unlock more and more objects to play with in the Toy Box, making your creations even more epic!

9

# HOW DOES DISNEY INFINITY WORK?

Welcome to one of the most high-tech video games ever made.

Inside your Disney Infinity Starter Pack you'll find:

**The game**

**Power Disc**

**Online code card**

**Play Set Piece**

## NEXT:

 **Plug the Infinity Base into your console.**

 **Insert the game disc.**

 **Switch console on.**

# BEGIN YOUR ADVENTURE!

The Infinity Base will begin to glow mysteriously. This is your cue to start. You can choose to play in the Toy Box or a Play Set. If you choose to play in a Play Set, you must place the Play Set Piece on the Infinity Base. This will unlock whichever amazing world you've picked and your adventure will start. Good luck!

**Disney Infinity Figure**

**Infinity Base**

# HOW DOES DISNEY INFINITY WORK?

Put a character from your chosen world on the left-hand-side slot of the base. For example, if you've decided to put The Incredibles Play Set Piece on the Base, you'll need Syndrome, Mr. Incredible or one of his superhuman family to enter The Incredibles world.

In the Toy Box, anything goes. You don't need a Play Set Piece, and you can use any characters you like.

## DISNEY INFINITY – CONTROLS

Making your way through the worlds of Disney Infinity will be a snap, once you know which buttons to push. Use this handy grid to learn all of the different things you can do. As long as you know which console you're using to play the game, just find the button that corresponds with the action you need, and you're all set!

| CONTROLS | XBOX | PS3 | Wii U |
|---|---|---|---|
| **ACTION:** JUMP | A | X | B |
| **ACTION:** FIRE WEAPON/ ACCELERATE VEHICLE | RT | R2 | ZR |
| **ACTION:** USE ITEM/ ENTER SPARK MODE | X | SQUARE | Y |
| **ACTION:** SELECT PACK/TOOL | RB | R1 | R |
| **ACTION:** AIM | LT | L2 | ZL |

## BUILD YOUR COLLECTION

There are currently six Play Sets to explore, plus more than 25 figures to play with, as well as dozens of Power Discs. There are over a thousand toys to collect from the Play Set worlds, which you can use in your own Toy Box worlds. Check out page 130 to see some of the coolest ones.

 Read on to get to know more about one of the most *INCREDIBLE* Play Sets in the game.

# THE INCREDIBLES
## PLAY SET

# Meet **MR. INCREDIBLE**

**Don't mess with the world's strongest Super dad!**

## SUPER TIP!

When in mid-air, speed towards the ground and deliver a powerful punch to any enemy or object directly below you.

*Oh, yeah! It's show time!*

# Unique Abilities

No Omnidroid on Earth can withstand *Mr. Incredible's brute strength*, especially if you smash his fists into the ground and send enemies flying. Syndrome had better watch out for Mr. Incredible's super-combo attacks.

# Strengths

Mr. Incredible's basic attack is a mixture of super power punches – perfect for denting those pesky Omnidroids. *He simply lifts enemies up and throws them away*, instantly destroying them.

# Gadgets

When behind the wheel, you can burn rubber in time-trial races, chase down bad guys and pull off some sweet stunts. *Or try out the amazing Wingsuit or Hover Board* and glide over rooftops with ease. Syndrome's going down!

Turn the page to meet *Mrs. Incredible*, who has her own unique abilities.

Mr. Incredible's wife has the power to stretch her body like elastic!

*We sure make a great team!*

## SUPER TIP!

If you're trying to climb across to a higher building and you fall short, quickly reach out and pull yourself to the top of the building you're facing.

# Unique Abilities

Mrs. Incredible can **reach places no one else can**. With her super-stretch skills, she can whip across town, yank objects closer and swing up buildings. Her long arm of the law can return blockheads to the park or criminals to the police station.

# Strengths

Mrs. Incredible is flexible, fast and fun. Her devastating combination of **super-stretchy arms and lightning quick** melee attacks means she can always flex her way out of any kind of danger.

# Gadgets

Whether you're picking the kids up from school or saving the world, one thing is for certain: you can do it a lot **faster behind the wheel of the Incredicar**. And, no doubt about it, hover boarding is definitely the new transport choice for Super mums.

▶ Read on to find out why Mrs. Incredible's son, **Dash**, is so awesome!

# Meet DASH

Small but super speedy, he's the fastest kid in Metroville.

Let's play!

## SUPER TIP!

Master the art of dodging and you'll move around the streets of Metroville in a blur.

GOT IT!

## Unique Abilities

Dash's *super speed* allows him to travel around the landscape in no time. He might be the smallest Incredible, but he's as powerful as the rest. He'll smash through anything that stands in his way when he's at top speed.

## Strengths

Even cars can't keep up with this Super kid. Steer Dash quickly out of harm's way and deliver a *series of hits and combination moves in quick succession*!

## Gadgets

Dash likes to *pilot the Incredicopter*. It's available in the Toy Store and it'll give you the perfect view of the streets below. If taking to the skies is too risky, then simply grab the Hover Board.

Turn over to find out why Dash's big sister, *Violet*, is amazing to play!

# Meet **VIOLET**

This is definitely not your average teenager . . .

*Looking for adventure? Right this way!*

### SUPER TIP!

Make sure you re-set Violet's force field every time it takes a hit.

6

GOT IT!

## Unique Abilities

You can't hurt what you can't hit, which is why Violet's **powerful force field** is supremely effective. Even the Omnidroids' missile attacks can't break it. Her power of invisibility also comes in handy for avoiding trouble.

## Strengths

Looks can be deceiving and Violet uses that to her advantage – this is one girl not to be picked on. Show the pesky Omnidroids who's boss by inflicting a **powerful blast** from the air, blowing the baddies to pieces.

## Gadgets

Glide around Metroville as a Super teenage pilot. Violet can take to the skies in the Incredicopter or the Glider. Not only do they get her out of harm's way, they're **perfect for grabbing hard-to-reach items**.

 Read on to learn about the Incredibles' arch-enemy, *Syndrome*!

# Meet SYNDROME

**The flame-haired baddie is out to take over Metroville.**

*I can feel my power increasing!*

## SUPER TIP!

Syndrome has no natural superpowers and is not always the quickest when moving around. So get him the Glider and take to the skies.

GOT IT!

# Unique Abilities

Syndrome is his name and scheming is his game. This would-be villain **makes good use of his huge brain** when it comes to defending himself. There are also a few combos he can learn when training at the headquarters.

# Strengths

His main assets are his major intelligence and unwavering determination to bring down the Incredibles. He also **packs one heck of a punch** that can knock anyone off balance.

# Gadgets

Syndrome has definitely got a few tricks up his sleeve. Purchase the Zero Point Energy Gauntlet from the Toy Store and you'll be able to **effortlessly pick up and throw blockheads, cars and other objects** on to surrounding rooftops.

▶ Take Syndrome to the streets and get ready **to battle evil with evil**!

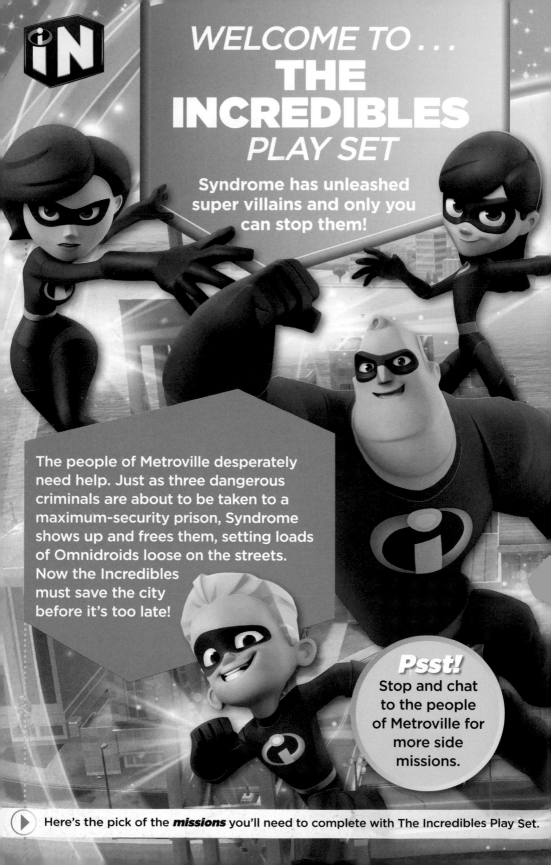

# WELCOME TO . . .
# THE INCREDIBLES
## PLAY SET

Syndrome has unleashed super villains and only you can stop them!

The people of Metroville desperately need help. Just as three dangerous criminals are about to be taken to a maximum-security prison, Syndrome shows up and frees them, setting loads of Omnidroids loose on the streets. Now the Incredibles must save the city before it's too late!

**Psst!**
Stop and chat to the people of Metroville for more side missions.

Here's the pick of the *missions* you'll need to complete with The Incredibles Play Set.

# Getting Started

Syndrome helps three notorious criminals escape before launching the Incredibles far into the distance. Their arch-enemy then unleashes countless robots on the city. It's your job to make sure they don't take over.

# Mission Alert

Metroville is under serious threat. Make your way from the docks to the city streets, attacking a water tower en route and putting out an already raging fire, before tackling your first Omnidroids.

**TOY ALERT**
You can now buy Mr. Incredible's Sports Car from the Toy Store.

**GOT IT!**

# Mission Alert

Before Edna can arrive in Metroville, you need to clear the landing zone of robots. There are five in total and you'll need to climb a building to destroy them. You're on your way to unlocking the hidden base of operations.

500   200

## ● Mission Alert

You need to buy and build to reactivate the HQ. Purchase the bridge from the Toy Store before climbing up and along the Hall of Heroes building, paying close attention to the golden coins.

🪙 500  💥 100

**TOY ALERT**

You can now buy the Downtown Express Bridge, Training Facility and Supermax Prison from the Toy Store.

GOT IT!

## ● Mission Alert

You've brought the Hoarder to the Supermax Prison, but before he can be prosecuted you need to release his hostages. You can do this by smashing the five traps scattered around the pier.

🪙 250  💥 50

**TOY ALERT**

You can now buy the Forklift from the Toy Store.

GOT IT!

## ● Mission Alert

Two groups of pods need destroying – and quick! Each pod is made up of two large ones and six smaller ones. You'll need to scale the nearby buildings to smash all the pods to pieces.

🪙 500  💥 100

## Mission Alert

An undercover agent has been sighted by Syndrome. You must get them along to Edna's Costume Shop for a makeover to throw the villain off the scent!

 500  50

**TOY ALERT** You can now buy Edna's Costume Shop in the Toy Store.

**GOT IT!**

## Mission Alert

A Tank Omnidroid has landed on Big Island. It's more dangerous than regular robots, thanks to its crushing claw hands and powerful red laser. Throw objects and keep moving.

 500  100

**TOY ALERT** You can now buy the School Bus from the Toy Store.

**GOT IT!**

## Mission Alert

Baron Von Ruthless is living up to his name. He's placed four bombs around the fountain on Big Island. Quickly throw the bombs into the fountain to destroy them.

 500  100

### SUPER TIP!
The only way to destroy the Baron's bombs is to put them in water. This will be very important in later missions.

# WELCOME TO...
## The Incredibles Play Set

**SUPER TIP!**
You can use the Incredicopter to blast from the skies.

**TOY ALERT**
You can now buy the Incredicar from the Toy Store.

GOT IT!

## Mission Alert

Snoring Gloria needs transporting to prison. You need to locate the paddy wagon and guard it as it drives to the location. This is a fairly simple mission with some seriously great rewards.

2000    200

## Mission Alert

Baron Von Ruthless has transformed himself into a monster. Keep the Omnidroids at bay as you escort the final villain to the Supermax Prison.

2000    200

**TOY ALERT**
You can now buy the Zero Point Energy Gauntlet from the Toy Store!

GOT IT!

## The Final Showdown!

It's time to end Syndrome's evil game. You'll need to climb a building to find him. As soon as you're on the roof, you'll instantly come under attack. Throw robots back at the villain until he can take no more.

2500    300

# Chests/vault

**Use the correct figures to open these chests for Toy Box goodies!**

## MR. INCREDIBLE

**1** **LOCATION:** Small Island, near the bridge headed to HQ Island.

**2** **LOCATION:** Docks, second level of the first crane.

**3** **LOCATION:** National Supers Agency HQ, on the left of the HQ base.

## INCREDIBLES AVATAR VAULT: REWARD 1

**LOCATION:** Small Island, on a roof headed towards HQ Island.

## MRS. INCREDIBLE

**1** **LOCATION:** Small Island, on a roof headed towards HQ Island with the water tower.

**2** **LOCATION:** Small Island, on the grass area by the park.

**3** **LOCATION:** Big Island, by the bridge nearest HQ Island.

## VIOLET

**1** **LOCATION:** Big Island, in front of the fountain.

**2** **LOCATION:** Small Island, in the grass near the bridge headed to HQ Island.

**3** **LOCATION:** Small Island, on the ground near the intersection.

## DASH

**1** **LOCATION:** Small Island, on a street next to the Big Docks.

**2** **LOCATION:** Big Island, on the grass near the fountain.

**3** **LOCATION:** NSA HQ, at the back past the road.

## SYNDROME

**1** **LOCATION:** Docks, on top of the boat in the Big Docks.

**2** **LOCATION:** Small Island, on top of the building with the white antenna.

**3** **LOCATION:** NSA HQ, at the stairs in front of the statue.

## WELCOME TO...
### The Incredibles Play Set

# DON'T MISS

The Hover Board is only available in this Play Set. It's faster than driving and it'll come in handy later. Here's how to unlock it.

**STEP 1**

A science agent needs to activate his secret weapon hidden in the city. You have to get him there safely.

**STEP 2**

There's no time to waste. Pick up the green-haired guy and get behind the wheel of a vehicle to speed things up.

**STEP 3**

Omnidroids will appear as soon as you begin to activate the weapon. Stay close to the weapon and fight for your life.

**STEP 4**

The robots will keep coming. Simply throw a droid right back at them. That way you can damage more than one.

**STEP 5**

Once you've defeated them, the secret weapon will activate. Make sure you protect it until it's up and running.

**TOY ALERT**
You can now buy the Hover Board from the Toy Store.

**GOT IT!**

# THE INCREDIBLES' ENEMIES

## Syndrome

Once a fan of the Incredibles, this flame-haired evil genius is the reason Metroville is under threat. What happens is up to you.

## Omnidroids

Developed by Syndrome, these pesky robots will spin round, chase you and even launch super-deadly missiles at you.

## Melee Omnidroid

These 'bots will slice you to pieces with their scissor-claws. Switch to Mrs. Incredible and use a long-range attack on these guys.

## Ranged Omnidroid

The weapons droids will attack you from long range with rocket launchers or melt you into a puddle with flamethrowers.

## Tank Omnidroid

These powerful robots are loaded with a laser beam and have heavier arms to inflict more damage on you – if they can get close enough.

# PIRATES OF THE CARIBBEAN PLAY SET

# Meet JACK SPARROW

With his sword and pistol in hand, Captain Jack is ready to battle his merry way across land and sea.

## SHIVER ME TIMBERS TIP!

Pick up hidden treasure from objects by attacking them from above.

*Welcome to my crew, mate!*

9

# Unique Abilities

Jack is always ready for an epic adventure. The bounty-grabber comes armed with his *handy Flintlock Pistol*, perfect for blasting off locked doors or treasure chests, as well as blowing baddies across the seven seas.

# Strengths

Jack Sparrow's primary attack is with his sword, which can *slash pretty much anything*. It also scores valuable points with every successful attack. A quick sidestep will leave your foes lunging at thin air.

# Weapons

Even more points can be earned with the *Pirate Bomb.* Aim this at enemies, and BOOM! When you upgrade to a baddie-busting Blunderbuss, your enemies have nowhere to hide. Standard issue for high jinks on the seven seas.

▶ Climb aboard and start conquering the waves, mate.

Take control of the mutinous Undead Pirate across the ocean and on land.

> *On deck, ye crusty cockroaches!*

## SHIVER ME TIMBERS TIP!

Blast chests open with an attack to find hidden treasure inside.

GOT IT!

## ● Unique Abilities

Like Captain Jack, this pirate has **more than one attack to throw the enemy off**. He'll draw his Flintlock Pistol without blinking and finish his foes off with a few strikes of his trusty sword.

## ● Strengths

Barbossa is **a master swordsman** and pretty powerful. He'll defeat enemies and gather the collectables they drop, taking what he can without giving anything back.

## ● Weapons

Anything Jack Sparrow can do, Barbossa thinks he can do better. Just like Jack, he can **throw a Pirate Bomb at his foes**, causing chaos and destruction. Pirate swords and bombs are tools of the trade for this mutinous undead dog of the seas.

# Meet **DAVY JONES**

The ugliest and most feared pirate on the seven seas is on the lookout for souls.

## SHIVER ME TIMBERS TIP!

His wooden leg can slow him down. But master the dodge manoeuvre and Davy will roll back the years when it comes to getting around faster.

*It's time I rule the seas!*

## Unique Abilities

If the cunning captain of the *Flying Dutchman* is losing a battle, he'll quickly get out of the way of danger by performing a **swift jump and roll**. He's also superhumanly strong and controls the Kraken.

## Strengths

Davy Jones is a demon with his cutlass. Any enemy brave enough to fight him should **beware of the sword-fighting feats** and writhing tentacles of this villain. It's no wonder he's feared by all who sail the seas.

## Weapons

Only a fool would dare travel the seven seas unarmed, which is why you'll **never see Davy without his sword**. Attack baddies or bash chests and objects to earn those valuable points. Use 'em well and use 'em without mercy.

Look here, mate – you're ready to board the *Flying Dutchman* and set sail.

# WELCOME TO...
# THE PIRATES OF
# THE CARIBBEAN
## PLAY SET

### You're needed to help defeat Davy Jones.

Learn how to customize your very own pirate ship, the best ways to dispose of enemy pirates and how to harness the power of the mysterious Kraken's Bane. While most missions can be completed in any order, these are the ones you need to complete to finish the quest. The rest are just for fun and loot.

## Getting Started

Your first move sees you immediately under attack! Steer your rowing boat through the cannon fire to dock safely.

**SHIVER ME TIMBERS TIP**
*Follow the green arrow to the dock.*

## Mission Alert

Pintel and Ragetti are waiting for you on land. They'll lead you to where Mr. Gibbs is languishing in jail. Bust him out.

**SHIVER ME TIMBERS TIP**
*If you find a locked gate, try blasting it with your Flintlock Pistol.*

14

## Mission Alert

It's a race against Davy Jones to find the treasure map. Follow Mr. Gibbs down the rail to the map's hiding place.

**SHIVER ME TIMBERS TIP**
*Complete side missions for extra coins. You'll need them to buy stuff in the Toy Store, such as upgrades to your pirate ship.*

# IN

## WELCOME TO . . .
### The Pirates of the Caribbean Play Set

## ● Mission Alert

A captain needs a ship. You may have lost the map to Davy Jones' men, but Tia Dalma can help you. Get to her by purchasing a ship from the Toy Store for 600 coins. Don't forget to pick it up from the delivery platform.

**TOY ALERT**
**GOT IT!**
You can now buy the Player's Pirate Ship in the Toy Store.

## ● Mission Alert

Time to visit Tia Dalma. Once on your ship, Mr. Gibbs will tell you which direction to take. All aboard!

**SHIVER ME TIMBERS TIP**
Now you'll learn all about how to control your ship on the high seas. Practise with your cannons now – you'll need them later.

## ● Mission Alert

You've arrived at Pantano Bayou, and you must find Tia Dalma. Row to her home, blasting bomb-throwing turtles out of the way. Help Tia fix her statue, and she'll tell you how to track down the five pieces of the Kraken's Bane.

# Kraken's Bane 1

The first piece is right inside Pantano Bayou. Follow your compass to find a tricky puzzle. Rotate the pieces of the big statue into the correct order to solve it. The goal is to get the faces pointing the same way.

# Kraken's Bane 2

The second piece is on the other side of Demon's Cape. The entrance will crumble, letting you through. You have to make your ship look like a Royal Navy vessel. Enter the ship menu, and select the Royal Naval theme.

## SHIVER ME TIMBERS TIP

If you don't have the Royal Navy theme pack, head out into the open sea near Fort St Grande. There are Navy ships you can sink then salvage pieces from.

Your mission is to get to the top of the fort. Follow the compass and avoid the townsfolk. Be ready, Davy Jones' men are waiting with razor-sharp swords. Knock them off the edge of the fort to save valuable time.

Now you have to deal with **Maccus**, the ugly brute who stole the map from you. Once you've sent him packing, open the chest to find the second piece of the Bane.

# Kraken's Bane 3

**SHIVER ME TIMBERS TIP**
*Keep upgrading your ship with extra spe*
*boosters and sails to help in combat.*

It's off to the Shipwreck Shoals,
me hearty. Purchase the Voodoo
Cannon from the Toy Store to
take down nine ghostly ships.
Tia Dalma raises a shipwrecked
island. Search for the third piece
before it sinks again.

# Kraken's Bane 4

Another piece is at Dead Man's
Cove. Buy the Pirate Bomb pack,
and follow your green compass
arrow through all the junk and
locked gates. Let down two
counterweights to open a gate
you need to get through.

**SHIVER ME TIMBERS TIP**
*Sometimes, ledges are covered
with rubbish, which can be cleared
with a well-placed bomb.*

Find and place the cogs that
are scattered around the area.
Follow the green arrow to find
them all, but be careful! You're
not the only one looking for the
Bane. Davy Jones' scurvy crew
are after it too.

**SHIVER ME TIMBERS TIP**
*Every time you see a big 'IN'
button, press it.*

Once you've bested Davy Jones' men in battle, it's time to get climbing. Use the cogs to get the platforms moving, then jump from the lowest to the highest, to reach the top point where the Kraken's Bane piece awaits.

## Kraken's Bane 5

Sail your ship (customized to look as crazy as you like) back to Buccaneer Bay where Tia Dalma is waiting with important info. Watch out – you have to fight Davy Jones' fish men, turtle bombers and Maccus.

Listen out – the bell in the tower crashes to the ground, revealing the fifth and final piece of the Kraken's Bane.

**SHIVER ME TIMBERS TIP**
In these final battles, blocking is more important than ever.

# BACK TO YOUR LOCKER, JONES!

Make sure the Kraken's Bane is equipped on your ship, then get ready to take on Davy Jones. Your job now is to fire cannons at the *Flying Dutchman*, while fighting off other enemy ships and dealing with the Kraken when it surfaces.

## REWARD

Once you've sent Davy Jones down to his locker, you're rewarded with the fearsome Kraken Hammer. Add it to your ship and you can control the Kraken to sink enemy ships.

# CANNON CORNER

Check out the different types of cannon that you can blast.

## Flamethrower Cannon

Scorch any ship that gets too close.

## Broadside Cannon

Essential on any self-respecting pirate ship.

## Triple-Shot Cannon

Triple the power, triple the punch to blow your enemies out of the water.

## Long-Range Cannon

Lets you fire at far away ships.

## Voodoo Cannon

Perfect for defeating ghostly enemies.

# ENEMIES
## OF THE CARIBBEAN

The Pirates of the Caribbean Play Set
has the most enemies of all the Play Sets.
Here are some of the best of them!

### ● Clam Pirate

A common enemy found on most islands,
the Clam Pirate will become very familiar.
Don't worry – they're no match for you.

### ● Driftwood Pirate

This enemy carries shields. Wait for them
to attack, so you can block them and
bash them when their guard is down.

### ● Maccus

This hammerhead shark has a roll attack,
a Blunderbuss and a fearsome melee
attack. Dodge away before striking.

### ● Turtle Pirate

The Turtle Pirate will chuck bombs
at you, blasting through your health.
Throw a few bombs back.

# MONSTERS
# UNIVERSITY PLAY SET

#  Meet *SULLEY*

**James P. Sullivan's the name and pranking Fear Tech students is his game.**

*M.U. rules!*

## SNEAKY TIP!

This big monster often gets spotted around campus before he gets a chance to roar. Make sure you tread carefully to avoid being detected.

GOT IT!

## Unique Abilities

Fearless and fur-ocious, *Sulley has a deafening roar*. Sneak up on your target and unleash an eardrum-busting sound to break objects, reveal platforms and make those Fear Tech students run for the hills.

## Strengths

Sulley performs a *shoulder charge* with those big ol' hairy arms, smashing any objects or baddies out of the way. Despite his size, Sulley is very agile. Keep your health up by rolling and crouching.

## Weapons

Sulley loves nothing better than blasting Fear Tech trees and statues with his *custom-made Toilet Paper Launcher*. Don't forget Sulley's Paintball Gun, used to decorate walls or to stun university guards. More fun than a minibus of comedians.

Take the big furry guy around Monsters University and play a prank or two.

# Meet **MIKE WAZOWSKI**

There's never a dull moment with this little green guy.

## SNEAKY TIP!

Look out for the Mike's Car Power Disc. It's a rare one, but unlocks a wicked Monsters University Car to use in Toy Box mode.

*You are just the monster I need for this. Whaddaya say?*

## Unique Abilities

Mike can sneak and scare with the best of them. He can certainly produce quite an impact. Perfect his *powerful sitting attack* and you'll send your enemies flying. What more do we need to say? Mike's a total and utter blast.

## Strengths

Study being sneaky or just let Mike perform his signature jig. He may not have the loudest voice, but he sure makes up for it with his *megaphone. Use it to scare rival monsters.*

## Weapons

When he's not busy redecorating Monsters University with the Toilet Paper Launcher, he's splatting it all sorts of colours with the Paintball Gun. And, if he's in need of a quick getaway, the *Beastly Bike can be used to get around*. Watch those little legs go.

▶ You're now ready to take on monsters of all shapes and sizes and get scaring.

# Meet **RANDY**

He's the craftiest guy in the Monsters University Play Set.

## SNEAKY TIP!

Randy is perfect for any missions that involve creeping around Fear Tech's campus without being spotted.

Name's Randy Boggs, scaring major.

# Unique Abilities

Randy has the ability to *make himself completely invisible* at the touch of a button, which means he can tiptoe behind security guards before scaring the living daylights out of them.

# Strengths

On the rare occasions he's seen during one of his stealth attacks, Randy has the *ability to slip out of harm's way.* Learn how to quickly dash to safety, then you can plan your revenge attack.

# Weapons

Randy is in his element when it comes to pranking other monsters. The *Hand Prank* from the Toy Store is one of his favourite ways to give himself a good chuckle. Set it up to give passers-by a giant slap in the face.

Take this villain around campus for some serious sneaking and scaring.

# WELCOME TO ...
# THE MONSTERS UNIVERSITY
## PLAY SET

**Rival campus Fear Tech is up to no good.**

These are just some of the monstrously cool things you can do during your time at Monsters University. Stop and chat to fellow students to complete all the scary side missions.

20

## ◯ *Getting Started*

As soon as you arrive on campus you're introduced to rivals Fear Tech. It's up to you to show the tricksy monsters you mean business and become the best scarer that Monsters University has ever seen.

## ● *Mission Alert*

Your first job is to take down some Fear Tech standees that have been littered around Monsters University by your rivals. Shoulder charge all five and reclaim the grounds.

 25  20

## ● *Mission Alert*

In order to pass Monsters University, you need to learn to scare properly. This is a lesson on how to sneak up on your target without detection and scare the wits out of them.

200 50

WELCOME TO . . .
## The Monsters University Play Set

## ● Mission Alert

Monsters University has been the butt of Fear Tech's jokes for too long and it's payback time. Open the entrance to the rival campus by shooting four targets with the Toilet Paper Launcher and start getting your own back.

**TOY ALERT**
You can now purchase the Toilet Paper Launcher in the Toy Store to complete the mission.

GOT IT!

## ● Mission Alert

Put your newly honed skills to good use around Fear Tech. Shoot two of their statues with the Toilet Paper Launcher. Be careful, Fear Tech students closely guard the statues.

● 250 ● 35

### SCARY TIP!
Fire at the statue when chased, but be careful not to get hit too much, or you'll end up in the 'locked room'.

## ● Mission Alert

Show some school pride and earn major tokens by decorating the Fear Tech campus blue. Climb up to the roof and grind across the high wires, unrolling Monsters University banners along the way.

● 200 ● 30

### SCARY TIP!
The student is partially invisible, which makes it hard to locate. Hang out by the back of the School of Botany building and you'll spot your target.

 ## Mission Alert

Terry and Terri have gone missing, but a student knows where they are. Carefully sneak up and scare the life out of the monster so it spills the beans.

300 40

 ## Mission Alert

Search high and low for 20 Fear Tech posters and decorate them with your handy Paintball Gun. The quickest way is on foot, using the shoulder charge to dash around the campus.

1000 100

 ## Mission Alert

Three Fear Tech students are roaming around Monsters University like they own the place. Scare them all the way back to their campus before they think trespassing is acceptable.

300 10

**TOY ALERT**
*The Breaking News Ender can now be purchased in the Toy Store.*

GOT IT!

# WELCOME TO . . .
## The Monsters University Play Set

## ● Mission Alert

Terry and Terri are out for a little revenge. As night falls you're tasked with letting off some fireworks into the Fear Tech dorms. Scare the guards before equipping your backpack from the Toy Store. Sneak and repeat.

🪙 300  ✴ 35

## ● Mission Alert

Hop on Archie the Scare Pig and get him back to campus. Randy tries to help, but you can do this without him. You need to smash seven statues on your way back to keep the pesky Fear Tech students busy.

🪙 1000  ✴ 100

**TOY ALERT**
You can now buy Archie the Scare Pig from the Toy Store.

**GOT IT!**

## SCARY TIP!

You'll probably be spotted by a guard on your dash around campus, but don't panic. Archie is fast enough to avoid getting hit so just stay focused on smashing those statues.

# ● Chests/vault

*Unlock Toy Store goodies by using the correct character from the Monsters University Play Set.*

## SULLEY

**1** LOCATION: Monsters University campus, on the wooden platform on the Clock Tower.

**2** LOCATION: Fear Tech, at the front of the Health and Phys. Ed. building.

**3** LOCATION: Frat Row, on top of the GRR house.

## MIKE

**1** LOCATION: Library roof, Monsters University campus.

**2** LOCATION. Fear Tech, on the roof of the Door Design school.

## RANDY

**1** LOCATION: Dorm roof, Monsters University campus.

**2** LOCATION: Fear Tech, on the roof of the Scare School.

**3** LOCATION: Frat Row, at the end of the bike trail.

## Monsters Avatar Vault: Reward 1

LOCATION: Clock tower base, Monsters University campus.

# DON'T MISS

During your time roaming the Monsters University campus you'll spot some Monsters University banners lurking about. This special mission is well worth your while.

# SCARY TIP!

There are 20 banners in total. They're scattered all around campus, in bushes, on rooftops and on ledges.

# ● Monster Tip

The mission will start when you collect your first banner and can only be completed when you've unlocked the Clock Tower area.

🌀 1000    ✦ 350    **Glow Urchin**

## TOY ALERT
You can now buy the Glow Urchin from the Toy Store.

**GOT IT!**

# ENEMIES AT
## MONSTERS UNIVERSITY

### ● Randy

After being humiliated by Sulley in the Scare Games, Randy joins ROR, a rival fraternity. His main weapon is his unique camouflage ability, which means he can sneak up on other monsters and can roam about rival campuses without fear. He's sly, cunning and very definitely not to be trusted!

### ● Fear Tech Students

The Monsters University Play Set may be all about pranking and scaring, but these guys are frighteningly dedicated to their cause. They won't hesitate to strike out and hit you, especially if you're trying to decorate their prized statues with the Toilet Paper Launcher.

# CARS PLAY SET

Piston Cup legend Lightning McQueen is one of the fastest cars on the track!

## RACING TIP!

You can purchase Missiles and a very cool Machine Gun for Lightning McQueen from the Toy Store to help beat his rivals.

*I'm ready to roll!*

5

GOT IT!

## Unique Abilities

Lightning's completely fearless. You can add some serious *turbo to his wheels* by visiting the Toy Store. If you find yourself driving in the wrong direction, Lightning will perform a swift turn mid-air, no matter how super fast you're going.

## Strengths

Lightning McQueen prides himself on his *speed and racing ability*. There's not a corner he won't turn or a jump he won't attempt, and any slowcoaches had better watch out for his ear-splitting horn.

## Weapons

Speed is this car's weapon, although his Tow Chain comes in handy too. Hook a nearby car and sling your catch wherever you want. Visit the Toy Store and you'll find a *Towable Wrecking Ball* – perfect for causing chaos en route to victory in the Destruction Derby.

▶ Start your engine – you're ready to race around Radiator Springs.

**High-tech Holley is a stylish secret agent!**

**RACING TIP!**

Master drifting to gain nitro boosts.

*I'm ready for my next assignment!*

## Unique Abilities

Holley is as sharp as she looks. Despite having some of the **fastest wheels in the desert**, you won't see Holley spinning out of control. If you're feeling really brave, try grinding along some rails as you're about to drive over the edge.

## Strengths

It'll take more than a few dirty tricks to get this classy car off the road. Holley's got the **charm and the very latest technology and gadgets** to outwit other vehicles. Plus she's trained for any terrain.

## Weapons

Add the awesome **Machine Gun** to Holley's gleaming chassis to earn some Hit Points at the touch of a button. If you're looking to climb some hard-to-reach places, get yourself the Towable Ramp and take it anywhere you want.

Shift into top gear with this sassy secret agent!

# Meet **MATER**

He might look ready for the scrapheap, but this top tow truck has a lot of life in him yet.

## RACING TIP!

Mater can get a bit forgetful in his old age, but he can still change direction in a split second.

*Tow Mater, at your service.*

# Unique Abilities

Mater might be a bit rusty, but he can scale new heights with the help of the **Towable Ramp**. Purchase it from the Toy Store and drag it to anywhere in the desert. Trusty old Mater is one of the most helpful vehicles in the Cars Play Set.

# Strengths

This old fella can mix it with the best of 'em. Move up the gears to show the young cars how it's done. Mater is **an expert at towing**: if something is in your way, don't drive round it – hook it and launch it.

# Weapons

Mater's still got power under his hood. Towing anything and everything won't cause much chaos – until you get hold of the **Towable Wrecking Ball** and throw it at something. Spruce Mater up with a set of Monster Truck Tyres from the Toy Store.

Blow the dust off and get Mater zooming around the desert again.

This Italian stallion thinks he's the hottest thing since wheels were invented.

## RACING TIP!

Make sure Francesco concentrates on the task at hand rather than on admiring himself.

*Francesco is here! No need to hold your applause.*

## Unique Abilities

He's the sleek Italian car with some serious firepower. If Francesco sees a rail that's worth grinding to impress, you can guarantee he'll take the opportunity. *Perfect drifting round corners* to get the edge on all the other racers.

## Strengths

Is he as good as he thinks he is? Well, yes. With his *high-speed racing and gadgetry*, Francesco zips around and still has enough juice for showing off. He'll zoom even faster if you purchase the **Turbo** from the Toy Store.

## Weapons

Attach the *Towable Wrecking Ball* from the Toy Store and watch him use it against opponents just for fun. The *Machine Gun* can also do serious damage. And, if that isn't enough, how about a *Missile*? Add it to Francesco's already impressive arsenal.

Rev your engine and take Europe's finest racer out for a spin!

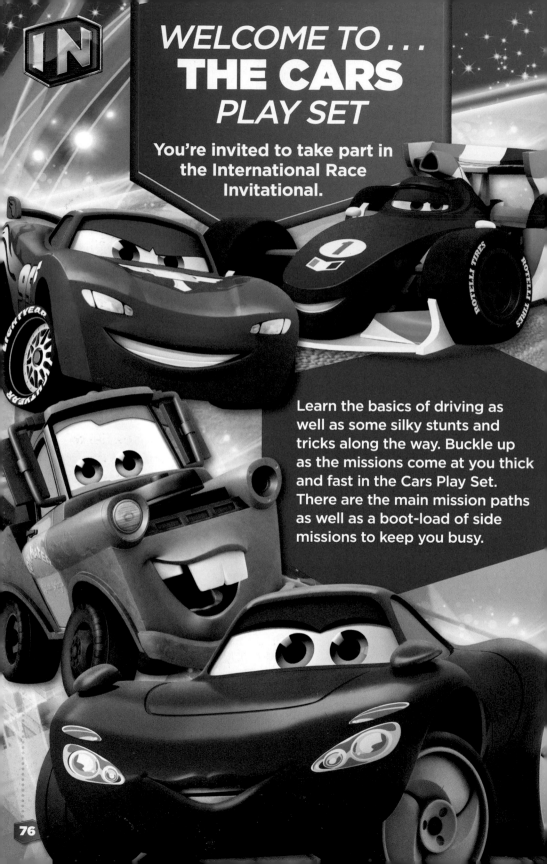

# WELCOME TO . . .
## THE CARS
### PLAY SET

You're invited to take part in the International Race Invitational.

Learn the basics of driving as well as some silky stunts and tricks along the way. Buckle up as the missions come at you thick and fast in the Cars Play Set. There are the main mission paths as well as a boot-load of side missions to keep you busy.

# Getting Started

Before you can let loose tearing around the sand, you need to find Luigi. He'll give you a mission to learn the basics of driving. It might not be the speediest of starts, but you need to know how to control your vehicle to succeed.

## Mission Alert

**CHALLENGE AVAILABLE**
Radiator Cap Race

Flo wants something special to get her café noticed. And there's nothing like an awesome jump to get people talking. Press the big green button by driving straight into it. Then rev your engine and prepare for serious lift-off.

## Mission Alert

Flo's mailbox has been knocked over by some careless drivers. Get her a new one by locating a red capsule then drive back to Flo's Café and select Flo's Mailbox from the Decorate menu.

 250  50

## ● Mission Alert

Radiator Springs is attracting a lot of attention. You're activated as an agent by C.H.R.O.M.E. but you've got to prove you can cope with the training programme. You're put to the test to show you can jump, turn and side bash.

⚡ 50  ✦ 50

**TOY ALERT**
You can now buy the Missiles Challenge from the Toy Store.
**GOT IT!**

## ● Mission Alert

**TOY ALERT**
You can now buy the Tow Chain Level 3 from the Toy Store!
**GOT IT!**

Ramone's trying out for a new reality show, but he's missing his premium paint cans. Use the compass to collect ten hidden paint cans. This mission should be straightforward, although a few cans are on higher ledges.

⚡ 200  ✦ 100

## ● Mission Alert

**TOY ALERT**
You can now buy the Cozy Cone Motel from the Toy Store.
**GOT IT!**

The King and Luigi need a car to race. Take up the challenge and try out the first real race on the new track. Be sure to start with a full turbo boost and drift into each corner. Avoid the obstacles or they'll cost you precious time.

⚡ 300  ✦ 75

## CHALLENGE AVAILABLE
Race Track A Forward.

## Mission Alert

Luigi's brand-new track is attracting all the international racers. Grab the turbo-boosting cans and hit the ramps to launch yourself to the top level. You'll find even more cans to collect, but don't crash trying to get them!

300 75

**TOY ALERT**
You can now buy Monster Truck Tyres from the Toy Store.

## CHALLENGES AVAILABLE

Radiator Stunt Score and Stunt Park Score, and, for Mater only, Extended Time Stunt (after purchasing Full Pipe).

## CHALLENGES AVAILABLE

Race Track B Forward, Battle Race Track B, and Monster Truck Race in Radiator Springs (if Monster Truck Tyres have been purchased).

## Mission Alert

A famous stunt car is in town and you need to pull off some cool tricks to grab their attention. The goal is to earn 3,000 points in just 90 seconds. Ramone's Body Art Shop is a good place to start.

500 100

**TOY ALERT**
You can now buy the Full Pipe in the Toy Store.

## Mission Alert

A storm is brewing and the tractors are seriously scared. You need to help them get out of the rain by towing them safely to the Barn. Get all five of them out of harm's way and the storm will blow over.

300 100

## WELCOME TO . . .
### The Cars Play Set

**CHALLENGES AVAILABLE**
Race Track B Reverse and Battle Race B Reverse (after purchasing Missile Challenge).

## ● Mission Alert

You're up against Shu Todoroki and you need to go backwards all the way. Get familiar with the racetrack and cut any corner you can. The ramps might be fun, but the turbo boost is more effective.

500 100

## ● Mission Alert

Fillmore thinks he's come up wit the ultimate fuel. Help him out by gathering the three spicy red peppers that are needed to mak it. You have to attempt daring jumps and activate the Tow Chain in mid-air to be successfu

## ● The Final Race

It's the best against the best in this final race. Now's the time to put all the awesome skills you've built up to the test.

**CHALLENGES AVAILABLE**
Race Track C Forward and Race Track C Reverse, Battle Race Track C Forward (after purchasing Machine Gun Challenge), and Battle Race Track C Reverse (after purchasing Mine Challenge).

# Chests/vault

Unlock Toy Store goodies by using the correct character.

## FRANCESCO

**1** LOCATION: Town, by the tree behind Flo's Café.

**2** LOCATION: Connector Tunnel, at the entrance to the Stunt Park.

**3** Location: Stunt Park, right of the pathway to the Stunt Park.

## Cars Avatar Vault

LOCATION: Balcony, under the balcony.

## HOLLEY

**1** LOCATION: Balcony, near the jumps.

**2** LOCATION: Stunt Park, left exiting the pathway to the Stunt Park.

**3** LOCATION: Town, near the road ahead of the Farm.

## LIGHTNING

**1** LOCATION: Old Road, on the top part near the middle of the railing.

**2** LOCATION: Town, on the ground near the Balcony and Half Pipe.

**3** LOCATION: Stunt Park, at the base of the Big Jump.

## MATER

**1** LOCATION: Town, outside Mater's building.

**2** LOCATION: Farm, in front of the Farm.

**3** LOCATION: Pathway to the Stunt Park, near the exit to the Stunt Park.

**WELCOME TO . . .**
**The Cars Play Set**

## DON'T MISS

Once you've cleared the caves you'll open up a new track, which unlocks the Turbo Level 1. You'll wonder how you ever drove so slowly before. Plus, it'll come in handy for completing trickier races later on.

**RACING TIP**

To complete this mission you need to get first place. It's not the hardest track, but it's one of the most important races you'll face.

**RACING TIP**

While the race is counting down, keep tapping the Accelerate button to get off to a flying start.

**RACING TIP**

Drift round the bends to ensure you stay in the lead. There's an alternate route through the caves that will give you the edge.

## CHALLENGES AVAILABL

Cave Race and Cave Battle (when Machine Gun Challenge is purchased).

**TOY ALERT**
You can now buy the Turbo Level 1 from the Toy Store.

**GOT IT!**

**RACING TIP**

Drift round the corners then, as soon as you see a straight bit of track, hit the turbo and leave your opponent in the dust.

# MISSION GIVERS

The Cars Play Set offers many different types of missions. Here's what to expect for each car.

## ● Flo

She'll give you a cool mixture of towing, combat and building missions early on in the game.

## ● Luigi

His missions are pretty straightforward and won't reap huge rewards. It's a good way to get used to the various different task types.

## ● Finn McMissile

Situated in the northwest part of town, you can often stay one step ahead of Finn by purchasing toys before he tells you to.

## ● Chick Hicks

This guy is hell-bent on racing. Chick'll give you plenty of track-based missions to see how good you are when the pressure's on.

## ● Ramone

His missions vary from decorating to collecting to delivery. One thing's for sure, though: you unlock a bunch of toys by completing them.

## ● Fillmore

A lot of this van's missions invo⋯ helping others. You can help Fillmore come up with a new fuel or help some scaredy-cat tractors.

16

# THE
# LONE RANGER
# PLAY SET

Saddle up. It's time
to ride for justice.

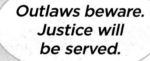

*Outlaws beware.
Justice will
be served.*

## SMART-SHOOTING TIP!

Break Silver into a
lightning-fast sprint to get
you across the map in no
time. Ride 'em out.

15

## Unique Abilities

The Lone Ranger has his trusty horse, Silver, ready at the touch of a button. And when you unlock the Constitution Train you can arm it with **Gatling guns and cannons** and lay waste to Cavendish's men. BOOM!

## Strengths

The Ranger has a powerful collection of attacks. He has a mighty punch that sends enemies, barrels or horses flying. Use your **climbing, riding and bullet-ricocheting skills** to bring justice to Colby.

## Weapons

Armed with his six-shooter, the Lone Ranger can take on all comers. And things get really explosive when he gets up close and personal with the **Dynamite pack**. Get ready for more fun than a rodeo of dancing cattle.

# Meet **TONTO**

**There's no one better for spiritual guidance across the desert plains.**

*Do not anger the bird.*

## SMART-SHOOTING TIP!

If you're surrounded by Cavendish's evil henchmen, let fly with your Tomahawks. They ricochet from enemy to enemy, so you can hit several baddies with one shot.

## Unique Abilities

**Tonto's horse**, Scout, lets him race across the landscape at incredible speed. When he teams up with the Lone Ranger on the Constitution Train, no wrangler is safe. Tonto also looks very stylish in his crow headgear.

## Strengths

A spirit warrior who is as fast as he is agile, Tonto can **throw his Tomahawks with deadly accuracy** and outride any outlaw who dares to trouble the town of Colby.

## Weapons

Tonto is armed with Tomahawks, which can shatter Butch Cavendish's men into a thousand pieces. He can also throw **Dynamite to destroy enemies** and remove any blockages on the train tracks.

# WELCOME TO . . .
# THE LONE RANGER
## PLAY SET

**It's time to help defend the Wild West.**

These missions are just a selection of all the awesome adventures you can have in The Lone Ranger Play Set. Make sure you talk to everyone in town for loads of fun side missions too!

# Getting Started

Uh oh, Butch Cavendish wants to take control of the railways. Everyone knows that whoever controls the railways controls the West. It's up to you to stop him in his tracks. Saddle up, cowboy!

# Mission Alert

You're under attack. Colby is being ambushed by five of Cavendish's men who are asking for trouble. Take them down with your six-shooter and complete the mission.

 500

# Mission Alert

The train engineer needs help. The saloon is on fire, and you need to put it out. Use your six-shooter to hit the water tower on the roof, flooding the fire out.

 100

## Mission Alert

After helping rebuild Colby, the train engineer needs you to clear the blockades that the Cavendish gang built on the train tracks. Use dynamite to blast the wagons away but beware an ambush from Cavendish's men.

**250 🔅 50**

**TOY ALERT**
You can now buy the Constitution Train Engine from the Toy Store.

**GOT IT!**

## Mission Alert

It's time to move out into the Wild West. Ride out to the ranch to deal with some Cavendish bandits and save the rancher. Now you can buy Silver from the Toy Box to help you get quickly around the map.

## Mission Alert

Time to upgrade the train. Signal for it to stop by shooting the switch by the track. Add any Train Cars you've unlocked in the Toy Box. Start with the Water Car, so you can get the needed liquid.

**100 🔅 20**

**SMART-SHOOTING TIP!**
Red arrows will lead you to battle missions, while green ones show you a destination.

# Mission Alert

Uh oh. The Sheriff has spotted Cavendish's men heading to the canyons. Follow your red arrows to hunt them down.

250 50

## SMART-SHOOTING TIP!
Don't forget you can double-jump when you're already in mid-air. You can even do this while you're riding Silver.

# Mission Alert

The telegraph is down, and the town is cut off. The Sheriff needs you to check the telegraph wire. Follow the green arrows to find the problem – pesky birds' nests! Blast them down with your six-shooter.

# Mission Alert

By now you should have unlocked various bridge parts from the Toy Store. Put them in place and make your way to Red's camp to find out Butch Cavendish's location.

 250  50

## Mission Alert

Butch and his men have escaped. Chase them to their camp near the railroad track, but bring the elephant. Buy it in the Toy Store and place it in front of you to trample their camp.

**250** **50**

## Mission Alert

The Camp Foreman will ask you for help. The Cavendish Gang is trying to stop all trains by destroying the Railroad Camp. You'll have to wipe them out to stop them.

**500** **175**

## Time for Action

It's time to deal with Butch Cavendish once and for all. Using the TNT Car on the train, blast the entrance to the silver mine. Butch has nowhere to hide. Climb the hills in the silver mine and lay waste to the gang.

### SMART-SHOOTING TIP!

There are also red targets to hit. When the green target reveals itself, switch to the cannon to finish it off.

# ◯ Chests/vault

**Use the correct figures to open these chests for Toy Box goodies.**

## LONE RANGER

**1 LOCATION:** Ranch zone, in the cemetery.

**2 LOCATION:** Colby zone, at the base of the spire.

**3 LOCATION:** Railroad Camp zone, across from the train station.

## TONTO

**1 LOCATION:** Comanche Elders zone, near the camp.

**2 LOCATION:** Red's zone, by the tall boulder in Red's camp.

**3 LOCATION:** Silver Mine zone, across from the sleeping man.

## Lone Ranger/ Tonto Vault

**LOCATION:** Colby zone, built into the wall behind the bank.

*WELCOME TO . . .*
**The Lone Ranger Play Set**

# DO_ _'T MISS

Once you've seen off Butch's men, earn the Crow Wing ability by collecting totems. This mission is completed throughout the whole adventure.

**TOTEM 1**

You'll come across this one while you're clearing the nests from the telegraph lines.

Find the canyon near Colby City, see off Cavendish's men, then head round the fire and into the alcove.

**TOTEM 2**

**TOTEM 3**

This one is right next to Red, by the Travelling Entertainments next to a brown building.

Find the miner. Look over the ledges near him and you'll see a boulder in the river. Jump down and the first ledge you come to has a totem.

**TOTEM 4**

**TOTEM 5**

This is at one of the highest points on the map. Head to the Railroad Camp and climb to the area where you found the Silent Warrior. Go to the left and up the hills. You'll see a tower; climb it to discover the Crow Wing pack.

# THE LONE RANGER'S E NEMIES

These dastardly types will stop at nothing to ensure the Lone Ranger and Tonto don't complete their missions.

## ⬭ Cavendish's Pistol Man

He'll pop at you from a distance. His bullets don't do too much damage on their own, but if you get caught in the crossfire of more than one you're in trouble.

## ⬭ Cavendish's Shotgun Man

Keep your distance from this guy. He's packing some serious firepower with his shotgun, which could really hurt you if he hits you. Aim carefully from a distance.

## ⬭ Cavendish's TNT Man

These clever villians will hide behind buildings, lobbing dynamite at you to blow you to smithereens. Throw some dynamite straight back. Ka-BOOM!

# TOY STORY IN SPACE PLAY SET

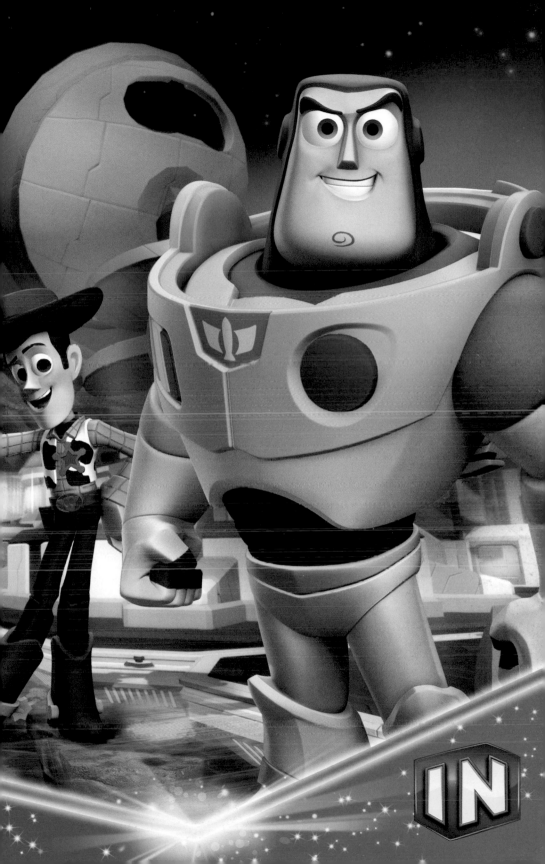

He's the good-natured toy cowboy who has a heart of gold.

*Sheriff Woody at your service.*

## COSMIC TIP!

There are various points on the planet where you can call Bullseye over, so if you're high up you won't have to struggle trying to ride him up there yourself.

# Unique Abilities

He might not be the strongest toy, but Woody has the courage of a true explorer. His shoulder charge **knocks villains through the air with ease**. And the Sheriff of Toys can really deliver a devastating ground-pound.

# Strengths

This cowboy can sure put up a fight. Woody has top-notch aim when it comes to **firing the Star Command Blaster**. Find your target on the mysterious planet and let fly. Shoot 'em up, cowboy.

# Weapons

What cowboy is complete without his trusty steed? **Bullseye is never too far away** from his best pal Woody. And don't forget to rustle up some serious fun with the Goo Shrinker. Watch your enemies shrink away!

Saddle up for fun at zero gravity. Cosmic adventures are guaranteed.

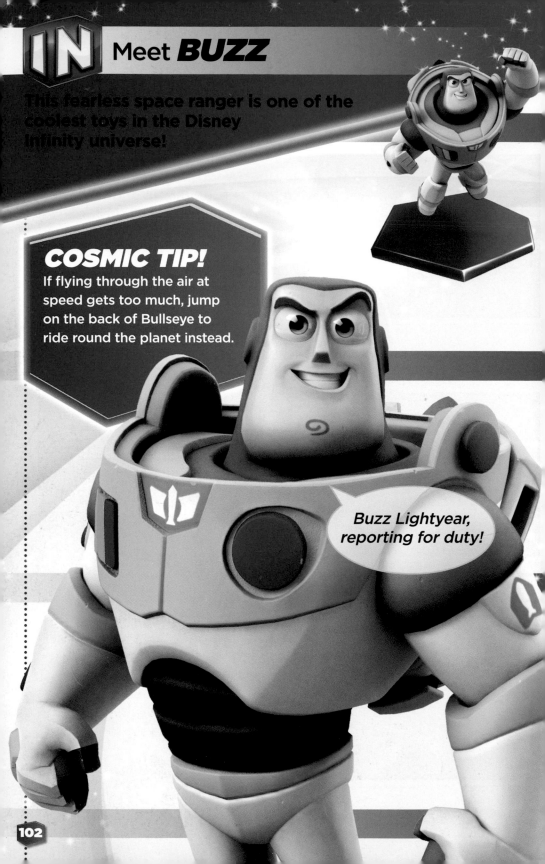

# IN Meet *BUZZ*

This fearless space ranger is one of the coolest toys in the Disney Infinity universe!

## COSMIC TIP!

If flying through the air at speed gets too much, jump on the back of Bullseye to ride round the planet instead.

*Buzz Lightyear, reporting for duty!*

# Unique Abilities

Buzz is in his element in this awesome space-adventure Play Set. He has a whole load of *Pixar Balls* at his disposal. Have fun chucking them at the hundreds of aliens wandering around the planet.

# Strengths

This brave superhero *performs a blistering shoulder charge*, destroying whatever is in front of him, including walls made of crystal. Even gravity can't hold Buzz back.

# Weapons

You'll never need to walk anywhere again once you've unlocked *Buzz Lightyear's Jetpack*. Plus it looks super cool. If that's not enough, get hold of the Star Command Blaster and fire your way through the Play Set.

Step into this space ranger's shoes for out-of-this-world fun.

**She's the tomboy toy who's quick on the draw!**

> *Somebody call for a yodellin' cowgirl?*

## COSMIC TIP!

Jessie likes being around others and can't stand to be alone. Call Bullseye over whenever you can – he'll not only keep her company, it'll speed the missions up too.

## Unique Abilities

Jessie is constantly cracking a grin (rather than a whip) and is a burst of athletic energy within the Toy Story in Space Play Set. She's also **great at getting herself out of any sticky situations** by performing a swift roll.

## Strengths

Jessie might not look like the strongest of characters but try telling her that. She'll produce a **charging attack as strong as anyone else's**. She's also an incredibly speedy shooter.

## Weapons

One thing's for sure: Jessie knows her way around a gun. Unsuprisingly, the **Goo Gun is this cowgirl's weapon of choice**. Shoot purple goo at Jessie's opponents and watch them shrink or fire green goo at them and watch them grow. Yee ha!

You're now set to tackle the challenges ahead on the mysterious planet.

# WELCOME TO . . .
# THE TOY STORY IN SPACE
## PLAY SET

**Help Buzz, Woody and Jessie on their epic journey far from Earth.**

You need to help the toy superstars relocate the Pizza Planet Aliens to a new home before lava from a nearby erupting volcano destroys their planet. Fly, jump and ride your way past villains and some incredibly tricky obstacles.

# Getting Started

You're under attack. A nearby volcano is erupting, spewing out hot lava and flying debris. You'll have to act fast to get all the Pizza Planet Aliens to safety.

# Mission Alert

Rex asks you to power up the tower to activate the Shield Generator to open up a force field. This will protect the local inhabitants from the nearby erupting volcano.

# Mission Alert

Hamm sets you the task of constructing the floor pads for the base by climbing up and jumping on the red button. It's a fairly basic start, but will set you on your way.

100 100

## COSMIC TIP!

Normal crystals are worth three coins. Gold ones are worth ten each. Grab 'em whenever you can to stack up the cash.

## Mission Alert

There's a mysterious cave filled with crystals somewhere on the planet. Locate the treasure trove and you'll be on the fast track to amazing riches.

 100  100

**TOY ALERT**
*The Delivery Platform can now be purchased from the Toy Store.*

GOT IT!

## Mission Alert

A clumsy alien has crash-landed somewhere on the planet. He's in desperate need of some medical attention – build him a hospital and get his bumps seen to fast.

 200  200

**TOY ALERT**
*The Hospital is now available to purchase from the Toy Store.*

GOT IT!

## COSMIC TIP!

It's definitely worthwhile crashing through the crystal walls.

## Mission Alert

Hamm has got himself stuck at the base of the volcano. Help him get to the peak, but watch out for flying debris as you go.

### COSMIC TIP!
Stepping on pink goo will shrink you, while green goo makes you bigger. Throw goo at things to change their size.

## Mission Alert

The green goo is flooding into a massive hole. Plug the volcano by smashing the ceiling to save the planet from destruction. Use the goo when smashing the supports.

 100  100

*WELCOME TO . . .*
**The Toy Story in Space Play Set**

## ● Mission Alert

Hop on the back of Bullseye for a race against time. There's less than a minute to gather up supplies to show that Bullseye has got what it takes to join the legendary cavalry.

**TOY ALERT**
*The Mega Pixar Ball is now available to purchase in the Toy Store.*

## ● Mission Alert

Once you've built the Egg Hatchery, have a word with Slinky. He wants to find out what's inside some mysterious shells. Deliver them to the hatchery and crack them open.

 50  100

**TOY ALERT**
*Star Command Blaster is now available from the Toy Store.*

## ● Mission Alert

Woody Wall

Wall

Slinky wants you to try out his Combat Simulator. Get inside an move on through the doors. Use your endless supply of balls and your charging attack to see you safely through the mission.

 250

Exit

GOT IT!

GOT IT!

## ● Mission Alert

The alien in the Woody hat wants you to paint a building to match him. Find the Decoration Set and customize any of your buildings with the Woody Wall.

 200 ⊙ 100

## ● Mission Alert

Chat to the alien with the Woody hat again and he'll set you the task of riding though a cave on the back of Bullseye.

 200 ⊙ 100

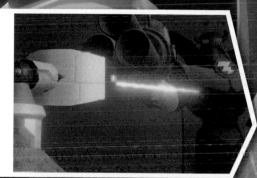

### COSMIC TIP!
Don't try riding Bullseye up to the high cave. It's much easier to get yourself up there and just call for him.

### DON'T MISS
Some boffins want to find out if they can use the goo to help their colony. You need to do some research. Use your Star Command Jetpack to whizz over the goo in no time at all.

🏅 500 ⊙ 100

### TOY ALERT
*Star Command Jetpack is now available to purchase from the Toy Store.*

GOT IT!

You have to gather 20 bits of green goo, all in the name of science. You need to destroy a Stink Spore to complete the mission. It's a long-winded task, but you'll be well rewarded.

500  100

**TOY ALERT**
The Goo Grower is now available to purchase in the Toy Store.

**GOT IT!**

## COSMIC TIP!
Stink Spores can only be destroyed by enlarged characters.

Your final task on the planet is to defeat the evil Emperor Zurg. He's grown too big for his boots so you need to shrink him down. Power up the tower by grabbing some batteries before blasting this evil baddie down to size.

## COSMIC TIP!
Take a dip in the green goo to grow bigger, then you'll be able to carry the battery to the tower.

# THE TOY STORY IN SPACE ENEMIES

When you take on Slinky's combat simulator, you'll encounter a whole host of baddies.

## ● Standard Zurgbots

They'll try to smash you to pieces with their giant robotic fists.

## ● Red Zurgbots

This variation will fire missiles at you that will send you flying. Be alert.

## ● Mini Zurgbots

These robots will launch a flurry of dangerous punches and rockets in your direction.

## ● Giant Zurgbots

The biggest baddies on the planet unleash powerful attacks with force-field rockets.

## ● Goo Zurgbots

Keep moving! These terrors will shrink you with pink goo given half a chance.

## ● Emperor Zurg

In the final showdown, you'll encounter this mega-bad guy. He wants to destroy the entire planet. It's up to you to stop him!

# ALL ABOUT POWER DISCS

**You won't believe the difference a Power Disc can make to your gaming experience!**

There are two kinds of Power Disc. **Circular Power Discs** give your characters special power-ups that can be used in the Play Sets and the Toy Box. **Hexagonal Power Discs** unlock special vehicles, gadgets, toys and skins for your Toy Box world. Some Hexagonal Discs give you a cool toy, and others allow you to customize the world around you. Read on for a selection of some of the coolest ones available!

Stack up to **two Circular Power Discs**, and up to **three Hexagonal Discs** on your Base at a time to increase the power of your upgrade!

## ⬤ SUPER-RARE POWER DISCS

**Dumbo the Flying Elephant**
Adds the Dumbo ride from the theme parks in the Toy Box.

**Abu the Elephant**
Adds the elephant version of Abu in the Toy Box.

**Astro Blasters Space Cruiser**
Adds the Astro Blaster vehicle from the Buzz Lightyear theme-park ride in the Toy Box.

# Hexagonal Power Discs

- **Stitch's Surfboard**
- **Dragon Firework Cannon**
- **Captain Hook's Ship**
- **Flamingo Croquet Mallet**
- **Mickey's Car**
- **Headless Horseman's Horse**
- **Cinderella's Coach**
- **Cruella's Car**
- **Astro Blasters Space Cruiser**
- **Parking Lot Tram**
- **Carl Fredricksen's Cane**
- **Calico's Helicopter**
- **Maximus (the Horse)**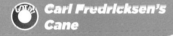
- **Tantor (the Elephant)**
- **Kahn (the Horse)**
- **Philippe (the Horse)**
- **Stitch's Blaster**
- **Condorman Glider**
- **Mike's New Car**
- **WALL-E's Fire Extinguisher**
- **Electric Mayhem Bus**
- **Angus (the Horse)**
- **Pizza Planet Truck**
- **Toy Story Mania Blaster**

Turn the page to see more *awesome Power Discs*!

**115**

## Hexagonal Discs

 **TRON Texture Set**

 **TRON Interface** *(Skydome)*

 **Tri-State Area** *(Phineas and Ferb Texture Set)*

 **Danville Sky** *(Phineas and Ferb Skydome)*

 **Frozen Flourish** *(Frozen Texture Set)*

 **Chill in the Air** *(Frozen Skydome)*

 **Marlin's Reef** *(Finding Nemo Texture Set)*

 **Nemo's Seascape** *(Finding Nemo Skydome)*

 **Rapunzel's Kingdom** *(Rapunzel Texture Set)*

 **Rapunzel's Birthday** *(Rapunzel Skydome)*

 **Victor's Experiments** *(Frankenweenie Texture Set)*

 **New Holland Skyline** *(Frankenweenie Skydome)*

**Jack's Scary Decorations** *(Nightmare Before Christmas Texture Set)*

 **Halloweentown Sky** *(Nightmare Before Christmas Skydome)*

 **King Candy's Dessert Toppings** *(Wreck-It Ralph Texture Set)*

 **Sugar Rush Sky** *(Wreck-It Ralph Skydome)*

 **WALL-E's Collection** *(WALL-E Texture Set)*

 **Buy N Large Atmosphere** *(WALL-E Texture Set)*

 **Alice's Wonderland** *(Alice in Wonderland Texture Set)*

 **Tulgey Wood** *(Alice in Wonderland Skydome)*

# Circular Discs

Emperor Zurg's Wrath

Merlin's Summon

Electro-Charge

C.H.R.O.M.E.
Damage Increaser

Star Command
Shield

Scrooge McDuck's
Lucky Dime

Churnabog's Power

User Control

Rapunzel's Healing

Bolt's Super
Strength

Violet's Force Field

Fix-It Felix's
Repair Power

Mickey's
Sorcerer Hat

C.H.R.O.M.E.
Armour Shield

Pieces of Eight

Ralph's Power
of Destruction

Dr. Doofenshmirtz's
Damage-Inator

## POWER TIP!

Play around with different combinations of Power Discs for unique effects. To unlock a sweet Spark Shield, combine the C.H.R.O.M.E. Armour Shield and Pieces of Eight Power Discs. When you get hit, you get sparks as a result, which helps you level-up your character.

How many have
you collected?

------------------------

19

# ALL ABOUT UNLOCKABLES/ COLLECTABLES

**There's loads of cool stuff to collect in Disney Infinity!**

## Capsules

These are the easiest way to unlock stuff. They're found in every Play Set and are very common. But some can be quite hard to reach.

- *Green capsules* contain toys and items for the Toy Box.

- *Red capsules* also contain items for the Toy Box that are primarily decorative.

- *Blue capsules* will be found in Play Sets and offer a gameplay hint.

## Vaults

In the Play Sets, there are a number of vaults with one character's image on them. *You need the corresponding character to open them*. There are also vaults with EVERY Play Set character on them – you'll need to visit these with each character. The vaults contain some awesome goodies as well as unique Toy Box worlds.

## The Disney Infinity Vault

This is the way you can unlock toys while in the Toy Box. Stand on the yellow pad on the Infinity Launch Pad to enter, and then spin to unlock goodies. You can earn spins in the following ways:

- **Finding green capsules** in the Toy Box Launch.
- Completing **Mastery Adventures** and **Character Adventures**.
- Levelling up characters. Each time you collect enough sparks to **level a character up, you get a spin**.

## Coins

During Play Set gameplay, you'll **earn coins by busting open boxes and completing missions**. These coins can be spent in the Toy Store to unlock items you need to complete the Play Set. Some of these can even be used in the Toy Box.

# WELCOME TO
# THE TOY BOX!

You've battled through the Play Sets and here's your reward – a Toy Box overflowing with landscapes, building blocks, toys and so much more. Now you can build, destroy, create and play to your heart's content!

You can **use any character within the Toy Box**, and they'll each bring their own unique personality. Sulley can still roar, Captain Jack still has his Blunderbuss and Mr. Incredible can still pound the floor to send enemies flying through air.

9

**Disney INFINITY**

- Incredibles
- Monsters University
- Pirates
- The Toy Box
- Options

To get the hang of the Toy Box, why not take a spin through some of the **in-game tutorials and Mastery Adventures**? These will teach you the basics, before you get stuck into the serious stuff. You can access these through the menu screen.

You'll notice that you don't have access to everything in the Toy Box yet. Why is that? Well, *you haven't unlocked it*. As you play through the Play Sets, you'll pop open capsules that contain random toys for the Toy Box. The more Play Sets you play and the more characters you use, the more you'll unlock.

# THE TOY BOX:
## *Getting creative*

**Look at some of the amazing creations that have already been made in the Disney Infinity Toy Box.**

Use your imagination to create Toy Box worlds that are every bit as incredible as these ones.

Now you know the basics of the Toy Box and have seen a few of the amazing things you can create, **_let's get started_** on some serious building.

# HOW TO BUILD . . .
## A Racetrack

**Start your engines and follow these easy steps.**

### BUILDING TIP!

Spark Mode is the easiest way to modify your track, as you can just delete or move pieces you aren't totally happy with.

## ● Step 1

Simply pick a blank Toy Box. You can also use a pre-built one if you want to race around some awesome ready-made landscapes.

## ● Step 2

Place your finish line. Search your Toy Box items for 'Race Track Start' and pop it wherever you'd like to begin.

### BUILDING TIP!

Track pieces are found between blocks and building sets.

# Step 3

Add the track. There are lots of cool types of track you can unlock. Take your pick from curves, splits, ramps, loop-the-loops and more.

# Step 4

Make sure your track is complete by linking the start to the finish line. You can either race round a circuit, or from point A to B.

# Step 5

Grab a friend, add a couple of cars and get ready for some high-speed fun. Get set, GO!

# HOW TO BUILD ...
## A Castle

**Why not try building something a little more advanced? A whole castle to play in!**

### ● Step 1

You can build a drawbridge out to space for a floating castle, or simply place your palace on the grass.

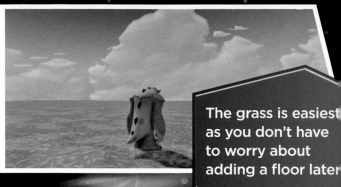

The grass is easiest as you don't have to worry about adding a floor later

### ● Step 2

You can use any type of blocks to make an entrance that's fit for a king or queen.

### ● Step 3

Add the outline of your castle using blocks. Make sure you leave some gaps for doors.

Exit Spark Mode    Move / Rotate

9

## BUILDING TIP!

Use towers and turrets from your Toy Box to make your castle even more royally impressive.

# Step 4

Build your walls up and up. It might take a little while, but you can make it as tall as you like.

## BUILDING TIP!

Try to unlock Castle Pieces in the Toy Box Vault to make your build look more noble and authentic.

# Step 5

Fill it with grand things or have some right royal fun and use it as a Paintball Arena.

# HOW TO BUILD . . .
## A Maze

**Read on to make a maze that you'll want to get stuck in again and again.**

## Step 1

Open up a blank Toy Box and decide what you want to use to build your mega maze.

## Step 2

The bigger the blocks are, the harder it will be. Whatever you do, try to make your maze totally a-MAZE-ing!

## Step 3

Lay out the exterior wall of the maze. Don't forget to leave a gap for the entrance.

# Step 4

Add the inner walls. Start from one side and work your way to the other, but be sure to leave a tricky route to the middle.

## BUILDING TIP!

If you notice there's no way to make it to the centre, just erase a block to clear a path.

# Step 5

Use a Creativi-Toy to trigger exploding fireworks as a reward for when you finally reach the centre of your maze. Good job!

# THE TOYS
## of the Toy Box

**Get your hands on these and you'll have a Toy Box bursting with adventure.**

Throughout your Play Set adventures you'll have purchased items from the Toy Store to help you complete your missions. These items are now available to you in the Toy Box. You'll have also collected several capsules (see p118).

There are over a thousand different items to buy, collect and use. Some are available from the start, others are collected via the Play Sets or by spending spins in the Disney Infinity Vault.

*Here are some of the best from each category:*

### Vehicles

| | |
|---|---|
| **GOT IT!** The Incredicar | **GOT IT!** Mickey's Car |
| **GOT IT!** The Incredicopter | **GOT IT!** Light Runner |
| **GOT IT!** Mule | **GOT IT!** Dumbo the Flying Elephant |
| **GOT IT!** Stage Coach | **GOT IT!** Recognizer |
| **GOT IT!** Silver | **GOT IT!** Mr. Incredible's Sports Car |

## ⬤ Creativi-Toys

*These awesome toys can be programmed to react in different ways when you touch them!*

| | |
|---|---|
| **GOT IT!** Area Light | **GOT IT!** Trigger |
| **GOT IT!** Bird's Eye Camera | **GOT IT!** Object Generator |
| **GOT IT!** Collection Pen | **GOT IT!** Power Switch |
| **GOT IT!** Energy Generator | **GOT IT!** Safety Dome |
| **GOT IT!** Falling Object Generator | **GOT IT!** Invulnerability Beacon |

## ⬤ Townspeople

| | |
|---|---|
| **GOT IT!** Tourist Van | **GOT IT!** Business Man |
| **GOT IT!** Tourist Truck | **GOT IT!** Cabin Boy |
| **GOT IT!** Wrangler | **GOT IT!** Comanche Warrior |
| **GOT IT!** Shopkeeper | **GOT IT!** Dragon Woman |
| **GOT IT!** Sea Dog | **GOT IT!** Dynaguy |

## ⬤ Enemy

| | |
|---|---|
| **GOT IT!** Fear Tech Paintball Player | **GOT IT!** Gator Goon |
| **GOT IT!** Fear Tech Student | **GOT IT!** Cavendish's TNT Man |
| **GOT IT!** Pig Goon Costume | **GOT IT!** Cavendish's Shotgun |
| **GOT IT!** Omnidroid | **GOT IT!** Barrel Costume |
| **GOT IT!** Melee Omnidroid | **GOT IT!** Shock Costume |

12

# THE TOYS
## of the Toy Box

## Building Sets

- **GOT IT!** Agrabah Palace Ramp
- **GOT IT!** Agrabah Palace Wall
- **GOT IT!** Agrabah Palace Wall Lookout
- **GOT IT!** Balcony
- **GOT IT!** Large Castle Floor

- **GOT IT!** Large Brick Building
- **GOT IT!** Metroville Manor
- **GOT IT!** Sandstone Building
- **GOT IT!** Shed

## Decoration

- **GOT IT!** Shipping Crate
- **GOT IT!** Rope Bridge
- **GOT IT!** Sandbag Barricade
- **GOT IT!** Red Mailbox
- **GOT IT!** Police Barricade

- **GOT IT!** Powerful Tiki Monument
- **GOT IT!** Newsstand
- **GOT IT!** Lamp Post
- **GOT IT!** Inflatable Guido Balloon
- **GOT IT!** Incoming Call Ender

# Track Piece

- Half Loop
- Rat Race Track Ramp
- Curved Rail
- Bump Rail
- Boost Pad

- Banked Race Track Turn
- Banked Race Track
- Arched Race Track
- Stunt Park Clover Pool
- Stunt Park Hill

# Tool/pack

- Sword
- TNT Pack
- Toilet Paper Launcher
- Toy Box Blaster
- Silent Warrior Pack

- Six-Shooter
- Pirate Bomb
- Hover Board
- Invisibility Device
- Flintlock Pistol

# Themed Terrain

- Construction Terrain 1
- Construction Terrain Corner 1
- Colby Terrain 1
- Sugar Rush Terrain 1
- Radiator Springs Terrain 1

- Radiator Springs Terrain 2
- Pirates Terrain 4
- Pirates Terrain Strip 1
- Monsters University Terrain 1
- Nemo's Reef Terrain 1

# THE TOYS
## of the Toy Box

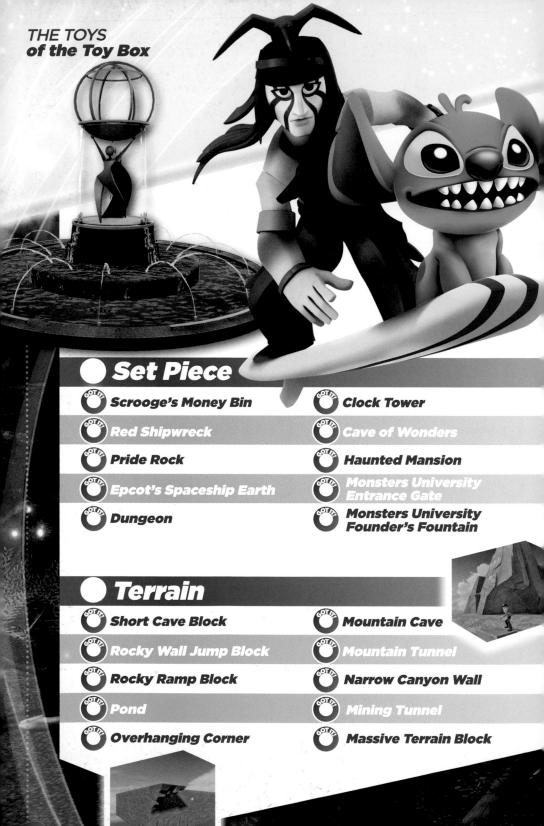

## ⬤ Set Piece

- **GOT IT!** Scrooge's Money Bin
- **GOT IT!** Red Shipwreck
- **GOT IT!** Pride Rock
- **GOT IT!** Epcot's Spaceship Earth
- **GOT IT!** Dungeon

- **GOT IT!** Clock Tower
- **GOT IT!** Cave of Wonders
- **GOT IT!** Haunted Mansion
- **GOT IT!** Monsters University Entrance Gate
- **GOT IT!** Monsters University Founder's Fountain

## ⬤ Terrain

- **GOT IT!** Short Cave Block
- **GOT IT!** Rocky Wall Jump Block
- **GOT IT!** Rocky Ramp Block
- **GOT IT!** Pond
- **GOT IT!** Overhanging Corner

- **GOT IT!** Mountain Cave
- **GOT IT!** Mountain Tunnel
- **GOT IT!** Narrow Canyon Wall
- **GOT IT!** Mining Tunnel
- **GOT IT!** Massive Terrain Block

## Sports Toys

- **GOT IT!** ESPN Banner
- **GOT IT!** ESPN Baseball
- ESPN Flag
- **GOT IT!** ESPN Goal Post
- **GOT IT!** ESPN Golf Ball

- **GOT IT!** ESPN Hockey Puck
- **GOT IT!** ESPN Bench
- **GOT IT!** ESPN Double Banner
- ESPN Basketball
- ESPN Soccer Goal

## Building

- ROR House
- **GOT IT!** Radiator Springs Courthouse
- **GOT IT!** Luigi's Casa Della Tyres
- **GOT IT!** Monsters University Registration Hall
- **GOT IT!** PNK House
- **GOT IT!** Newspaper Stand
- **GOT IT!** Monsters University Hall
- **GOT IT!** HQ Research Station
- **GOT IT!** HSS House
- **GOT IT!** Hotdog Stand

# HOW TO CREATE ...
## An American Football Game
### The perfect challenge for all sports fans!

### ● Step 1

Open yourself up a nice empty Toy Box with plenty of room to run around.

### ● Step 2

Set yourself some boundaries. Build a big rectangle from blocks or if you've unlocked the ESPN Sports Pack use stadium pieces.

### ● Step 3

Place an ESPN Goal Post at either end of your pitch, ready for some awesome goal scoring.

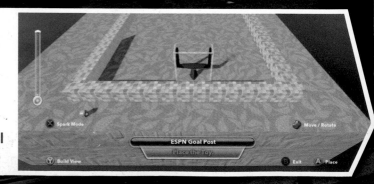

Make your own fun mini-games. Dig deep into the Toy Box and you'll find everything you need to get started. Just add imagination!

9

## Step 4

Put Scream Energy Launchers in front of each goal, making sure they're facing the right way.
Then add a ball to the mix.

## Step 5

Link up fireworks for when the ball crosses the goalposts, and play away. As soon as you move the ball on to the Scream Energy Launcher, you score a point. TOUCHDOWN!

Now all that's left to do is score a goal and watch as the crowd goes wild!

# HOW TO CREATE...
## A Flying Game

**Take to the skies and create your own flying game.**

### ● Step 1

Build or place a few things in your Toy Box that you'd like to fly round or even fire at. The more buildings you've got, the more fun your adventure will be.

### ● Step 2

Unlock vehicles or objects that can take to the sky. The Incredicopter is good for firing at things and the Dumbo the Flying Elephant Power Disc is fab if you want to soar high above your Toy Box.

## Step 3

Map out a route that would be fun to explore. Whizz around buildings, through caves and under bridges to really make the most of soaring around the Toy Box. Marking out a start and a finish is always a good place to begin.

## Step 4

Add some enemies that will cause you a few headaches along the way. Make sure you have some baddies that can throw things at you. You don't want it to be too easy. Hey, it's a game after all.

## Step 5

Once you've got your route and some things to avoid or collect, you're ready to fly. Race a friend to the finish line to make things even more exciting.

# HOW TO BUILD . . .
## A Platform Game

The Toy Box allows you to make your very own platform games. Here's how!

## ● Step 1

Simple platform games are a lot of fun and won't take hours to create. Grab yourself some building blocks and map out a start and finish to your very own adventure.

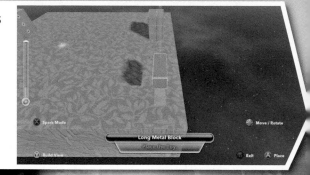

## ● Step 2

To make it really exciting you need some obstacles to overcome. You could try setting Bowling Balls on Repeaters – and then try to avoid them. It's totally up to you how hard you make it.

## ● Step 3

Add in some rewards and things to help you along the way. Add in Turbo Boosters to help you speed up and avoid those pesky enemies.

## Step 4

It's not much of a game if there's no one out to stop you so add some enemies. It'll be even more fun if you've got some things to bash up along your journey.

## Step 5

Link up a firework display to go off at the finish, so the whole Toy Box knows you've won the game. Hey, a little showing off never hurt – just ask Francesco!

20

# HOW TO CREATE...
## A Fighting Game

Ka-chow! If someone messes with you, there's only one thing to do – settle it with a good old-fashioned battle.

## ● Step 1

Why not set up the fight in the Toy Box Launch to give your battle the combat background it deserves?

## ● Step 2

Get ready to rumble. Pop a Side-Step Camera in front of where your combat will take place.

## Step 3

Set up two triggers: one to activate the Side-Step Camera, and one to turn it off again.

## Step 4

Place an Enemy Generator at the end of the arena ready for action.

## Step 5

Step on the Activate Switch trigger you linked to the camera earlier, and wait for the enemies to roll in. Or play with a friend and see who can destroy the other first.

# TOY BOX
## ADVENTURES

As well as the freedom to explore the Toy Box and create your own games, there are also amazing adventures to discover.

## ● *Character Adventures*

Each Disney Infinity character has an awesome adventure, 100% unique to them, in the Toy Box. To find it, choose a figure, put it on the Base, enter the Toy Box and then simply select their adventure in the menu screen.

**Lone Ranger's Justice Run**

Take out as many enemies as possible before the time runs out.

● Gold: 100 Points

● Silver: 65 Points

★ Bronze: 20 Points

⊗ Launch

### ADVENTURE TIP!

*Try playing in multiplayer mode to help complete the harder challenges.*

*Find adventures in the 'Travel' menu.*

These are bite-sized challenges that will earn you sparks and Toy Box Vault spins. There are all kinds of adventures to explore, so be sure to try them all.

# Mastery Adventures

These challenges show you how to get the best out of the toys, while earning you sparks. There are also Combat and Driving Mastery Adventures to really test your playing skills and show you're a Master of the Toy Box.

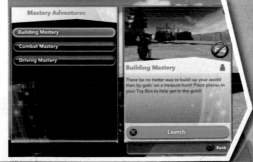

Mastery Adventures

Building Mastery

Combat Mastery

Driving Mastery

Building Mastery

There be no better way to build up your world than by goin' on a treasure hunt! Place pieces in your Toy Box to help get to the gold!

Launch

Back

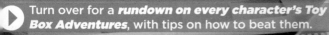

Turn over for a *rundown on every character's Toy Box Adventures*, with tips on how to beat them.

# The Incredibles Toy Box Adventures

Tick, tock. It's time to go on a super adventure!

## ● Mr. Incredible

You're up against the clock to destroy the domes and save Metroville. Use Mr. Incredible's amazing superhuman strength and take no prisoners when it comes to bashing baddies.

**SUPER HINT!**
*Omnidroids will block your way. Mix up your attacks to get past them.*

**SUPER HINT!**
*Try throwing all the crooks off the roof before delivering them to prison.*

## ● Mrs. Incredible

9

The police need a super-elastic hand. Use Mrs. Incredible's unique fighting style to return as many villains as possible back to where they belong.

## Violet

**SUPER HINT!**
The spotlights will get faster over time, so you'll have to get a wriggle on.

Creep around, avoiding the spotlights while grabbing as many collectables as you can. If anyone's agile enough to avoid detection it's this super-powered teenager.

## Dash

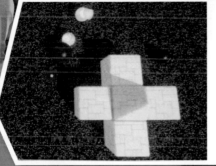

Dart around the Toy Box taking care to avoid the tricky red and blue balls while gathering as many collectables as you can. There's really no one speedier than Dash.

**SUPER HINT!**
You can't jump over the red balls, but double-jump and you'll leap over the blue balls.

**SUPER HINT!**
Take aim. You'll need to hit the targets to earn gold.

## Syndrome

Cause chaos with the most dangerous super-villain of all time by throwing blockheads around the rooftops. You'll earn more points every time you hit a bulls-eye. Hurrah.

**The pirates have their work cut out with these challenges.**

## ● Captain Jack Sparrow

Captain Jack's on the hunt for treasure. Round up as many collectables as you can. There aren't many people more crafty than Captain Jack so if anyone can succeed here, it's him.

### SHIVER ME TIMBERS HINT!

*Make good use of the packs and tools that are available. Star Command Boost Packs can fire you into the air, which can be a big help.*

## ● Barbossa

Time is against this master swordsman. Defeat the baddies and pick up the loot they leave behind. Barbossa always looks out for himself so he should have no trouble triumphing.

### SHIVER ME TIMBERS HINT!
*The key to this challenge is to never stop moving. The enemies will spawn in high numbers as you progress.*

## ● Davy Jones

### SHIVER ME TIMBERS HINT!
*Defeating the hammerhead-shark pirate on the upper pirate ship will earn you four points.*

The demon of the deep is doing what he does best, defeating enemies and making off with the treasure. He's up against the clock, but that won't faze this heartless captain.

# IN Monsters University Toy Box Adventures

**Get in training for some serious pranking on campus.**

## ● Sulley

His huge hairy arms come in handy as this lovable scarer blasts as many Paintballers as he can. There aren't many monsters more fur-ocious, so this should be a breeze.

### SCARY HINT!

*Timing is everything. If you stop to reload your gun, take the opportunity to shoulder-charge the enemy.*

5

## Randy

Tiptoe past the enemies and pick up as many collectables as you can. Beware of the timer counting down though – you haven't got all day to sneakily creep about.

**SCARY HINT!**
*Front rolls are a quick way of getting around. Pay more attention to the timer than the enemies.*

## Mike

**SCARY HINT!**
*Focus on the upper level platforms. Take time to look in every nook and cranny for launcher pranks.*

Just watch Mike go. Pick up as many items as you can on this sneaky dash. The red items are worth the most, the orange are the second most valuable and yellow are worth the least.

**Gear up for some pure fun on wheels.**

### RACING HINT!
*Performing tricks whenever you can will keep your boost meter up during Lightning's high jinks.*

## ● Lightning McQueen

Start your engine. Gather as many different coloured collectables as fast as you can. The red ones are worth the most, followed by the orange, then the yellow. Ready, set, GO!

## ● Holley

### RACING HINT!
*See enemies off in double-quick time by firing a missile, then crashing into them straight away.*

The stylish spy is back doing what she does best – destroying enemy targets. There's no time to stop and admire her work though! Pick up awesome new weapons as you go.

## RACING HINT!

*Don't be afraid to use a shortcut or two. There's one very near the start.*

● **Francesco**

The slick Italian has to complete three laps without wasting any time. He's got supreme confidence in his ability so this challenge won't give him any headaches.

● **Mater**

## RACING HINT!

*Memorize your surroundings to make it easier for the local yokel to deliver the Tourist Cars to their destinations.*

Keep on truckin' and help Mater tow the stranded Tourist Cars to their destination. There's no one more experienced at towing than Mater!

# The Lone Ranger Toy Box Adventures

**Those pesky outlaws won't catch themselves!**

## The Lone Ranger

Ride 'em to take out as many enemies as possible before the time runs out. There's no one in the Wild West with a deadlier shot than this masked man of justice.

### SHARP-SHOOTING HINT!
*Fire the Blaster as much as possible. Don't give the enemy time to even breathe.*

### SHARP-SHOOTING HINT!
*Each lap of the canyons will spawn fresh new enemies. Go straight for the ones on horseback and hoover up the points.*

○ *Tonto*

Get your feet movin' and collect as many pick-ups as possible in the given time. Magically turn Tonto into a crow and soar above the desert to try to capture the gold.

## SHARP-SHOOTING HINT!
*Focus on the red and orange collectables, as they're the most valuable.*

19

## SHARP-SHOOTING HINT!
*Press the Attack button to soar higher. You'll need to do this to grab some of the highest collectables in the challenge.*

# Toy Story in Space
# Toy Box Adventures

**No challenge is too big
for the superstar toys.**

## ● *Woody*

It's a race against time
for Woody and Bullseye.
You must complete
three laps of an
obstacle-riddled track.
It's not easy, but with
Bullseye's strength and
speed you'll be fine.

### COSMIC HINT!
*Use your Star Command
Blaster to clear objects
out of the way.*

## Buzz Lightyear

### COSMIC HINT!
To get around the map in double-quick time, use Buzz Lightyear's Jetpack.

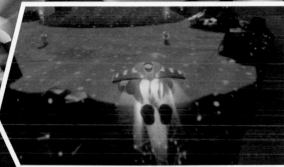

The townspeople are stuck in a host of meteors. Pick 'em up one at a time and take them to the Fetch Pen. If there was ever a time to prove Buzz is a real space ranger, this is it.

## Jessle

### COSMIC HINT!
Riding Bullseye will help you complete the adventure as he's quicker on his feet than Jessie.

The cowgirl has been called upon to get all the cute lil' critters back to the pen. You've got less than four minutes to get all the animals safely back.

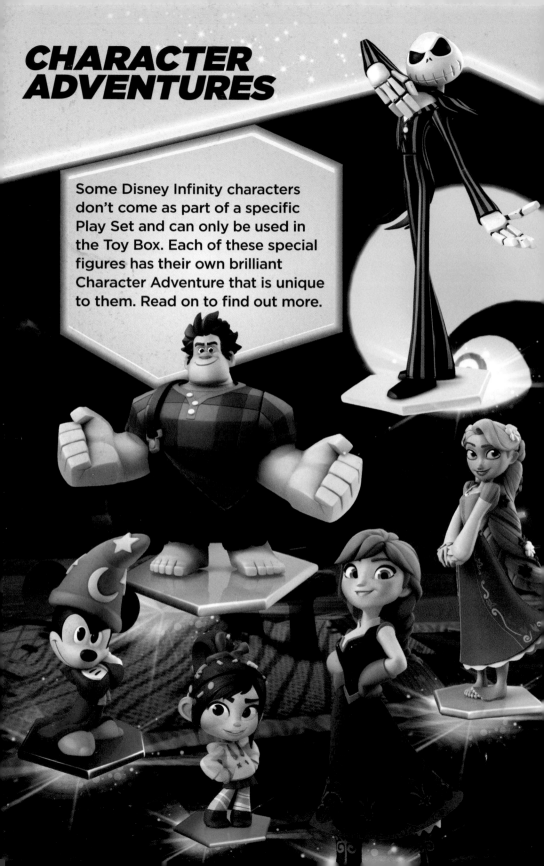

# CHARACTER ADVENTURES

Some Disney Infinity characters don't come as part of a specific Play Set and can only be used in the Toy Box. Each of these special figures has their own brilliant Character Adventure that is unique to them. Read on to find out more.

# Rapunzel
## Toy Box Adventures

It's time to let your hair down.

**GAME HINT!**
Don't forget to jump left and right to switch rails. It'll help you collect even more lanterns.

## Rapunzel

Every year, on Rapunzel's birthday, her parents release lanterns into the sky. In this race, you must collect as many floating lanterns as you can.

**GAME HINT!**
Sometimes you'll be rewarded for leaving the rails entirely. Explore the whole area on foot for extra sparks and lanterns.

# Frozen
# Toy Box Adventures

**Don't freeze! Get active.**

**GAME HINT!**
*The green arrow will point you to the nearest collectable.*

## ● Anna

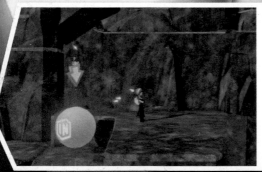

Collect as many objects as you can. Guide Anna across the icy landscape, using all your climbing and jumping skills, before things get really frosty.

**GAME HINT!**
*You only need 10 objects to earn the bronze award, so start off slowly.*

**GAME HINT!**
Keep moving between slingshots to get closer to tricky targets.

**GAME HINT!**
Aim carefully. Yellow targets are worth one point, while red ones are worth three.

## Elsa

Brrr! Time for some chilly target practice. Fire Elsa's sub-zero slingshot at the targets for some high scores. There's no business like snow business.

# Wreck-It Ralph
# Toy Box Adventures

Like knocking down stuff?
Then this is the
challenge for you.

**GAME HINT!**
*Throw a cherry bomb
to clear a path
through the blocks.*

## ● Wreck-It Ralph

Ralph's Cherry Bomb

There's a massive building
in your way and only one
way through – SMASH!
Grab as many collectables
as you can on your way.
You're gonna wreck it!

**GAME HINT!**
*You'll need the double-
jump to get the highest
scores in this sweet
adventure.*

**GAME HINT!**
*Dodge the dark brown squares or you'll end up stuck in the sticky chocolate for ages.*

# Vanellope

Rev your engine and burn round the track three times as fast as you possibly can. Just three other drivers stand between you and victory. You can do it!

**GAME HINT!**
*Don't miss the power-ups that are scattered around the course.*

# Sorcerer's Apprentice Mickey Toy Box Adventures

**Everyone's favourite magic mouse!**

## GAME HINT!

The more times you complete the adventure, the better you'll get to know it – meaning you'll be able to do it faster and faster.

## GAME HINT!

The blue pads act as respawn points. You'll appear here if you get knocked off the level by a giant mallet or other obstacles.

## ● Sorcerer's Apprentice Mickey

Mickey's Magical Castle has been surrounded by brooms. Brush up your skills and find a way out as quickly as possible.

# Jack Skellington Toy Box Adventures

## Join the Pumpkin King!

**GAME HINT!**
*Pick a strong weapon, like Buzz Lightyear's Blaster, to fend off enemies.*

## ◯ Jack Skellington

Trick or treat? Jack's nightmare creations have turned on him. Help him stay in one piece in the spooky setting, using all your packs and tools.

**GAME HINT!**
*There's only rule. Survive as long as possible.*

# GO ONLINE

*There's a whole new world waiting for you when you take Disney Infinity online!*

# ONLINE EXPLAINED

To really get the most from Disney Infinity's Toy Box, you'll need to go online.

## ⬤ Invite

Invite people into the amazing Toy Box worlds you've created. They can join your game or you can invite them to play cool adventures with you.

## ⬤ Upload

Upload and download Toy Box worlds to share the magic with people from around the world. Read pages 170/171 to learn more about this.

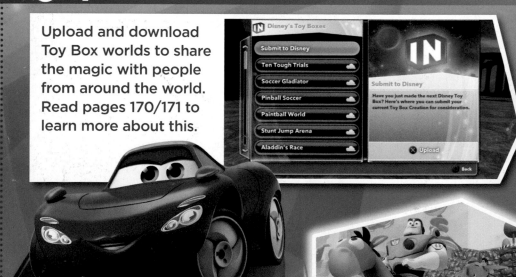

You can even share the Disney Infinity experience on your computer. Create a Disney Account and head to: *www.infinity.disney.com* to play the game online.

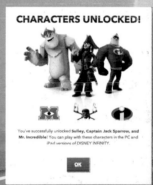

You'll find Web Codes on many pieces of Disney Infinity packaging. Simply log into your Disney Infinity Account and enter the code in the Redemption Box to unlock digital versions of the figures.

**NOTE:** You can only use Web Codes once.

# HOW TO SHARE TOY BOXES

**Sharing your Toy Boxes with the Disney Infinity world is easy.**

## To upload

Open the Pause menu and choose 'Online/Multiplayer'. Then hit 'Toy Box Share'. Follow the prompts, and the creation of your choice will be uploaded. Different challenges for themed Toy Boxes are being released by Disney all the time, so if one Toy Box doesn't make the list, just wait for the next challenge and try again.

**NOTE:** There's no guarantee your creation will be made available for others to download.

## To download

In the Toy Box Share menu, follow the options to download whichever Toy Boxes take your fancy and drop yourself right into the world. This is a great way to try out new toys that you haven't unlocked yet, and it'll give you ideas on how fun stuff like Creativi-Toys works.

**Check out some of the cool Toy Boxes you can download!**

**NOTE:** You must be connected to the Internet in order to upload/download from the Disney Infinity server.

# ONLINE SAFETY AND COMMUNITY

It's important that every Disney Infinity gamer knows they're playing in a totally safe environment.

**1** *Never share your personal information* with anyone you meet online. This could be your name, phone number, address or name of your school. Jack Sparrow would never reveal the location of hidden treasure to Barbossa, and neither should you.

**2** In Toy Story, all the toys need to work together to rescue Buzz from Sid's house. *Always respect others within the game.* Imagine you are in their shoes if someone asks you for help, and others will help you too.

**3** Keep your language clean. Any *offensive language could result in being banned* from Disney Infinity. If Sulley tried using any bad language, he'd be expelled from Monsters University straight away.

# I-SPY PUZZLE

## Can you crack the code and solve this brain teaser?

Hey there, Infinity fans. Did you spot Sorcerer's Apprentice Mickey throughout this book holding up random numbers? Write each number down in the order it appeared below, then use this handy code breaker to match the number to the correct letter of the alphabet. When you've got them all, they will spell out a special Disney Infinity phrase that describes the magic of the Toy Box.

\_ \_ \_ \_ \_ \_ \_

\_ \_ \_ \_ \_ \_ \_ \_ \_ \_

| A | B | C | D | E | F | G | H | I | J | K | L | M |
|---|---|---|---|---|---|---|---|---|---|---|---|---|
| 1 | 2 | 3 | 4 | 5 | 6 | 7 | 8 | 9 | 10 | 11 | 12 | 13 |

| N | O | P | Q | R | S | T | U | V | W | X | Y | Z |
|---|---|---|---|---|---|---|---|---|---|---|---|---|
| 14 | 15 | 16 | 17 | 18 | 19 | 20 | 21 | 22 | 23 | 24 | 25 | 26 |

# TOY ALERT CHECKLIST

Have you unlocked all the toys from the missions in this book? Tick them off here as you play!

 **Constitution Train Engine**

 **Triple Shot Cannon**

 **Edna's Costume Shop**

 **Flamethrower Cannon**

 **Voodoo Cannon**

 **Archie the Scare Pig**

 **Toilet Paper Launcher**

 **Player's Pirate Ship**

 **Turbo Level 1**

 **Glow Urchin**

**Incredicar**

**Breaking News Ender**

 **Hover Board**

 **Full Pipe**

 **Broadside Cannon**

 **Forklift**

 **Mr. Incredible's Sports Car**

 **Long-Range Cannon**

 **School Bus**

 **Zero Point Energy Gauntlet**

 **Missiles Challenge**

 **Tow Chain Level 3**

 **Monster Truck**

 **Downtown Express, Training Facility and Supermax Prison**

 **Cozy Cone Motel**

# TO-DO LIST

This page is for you to jot down notes of adventures you'd like to have, but haven't had time for yet.

## IDEA!

Why not add a cauldron to a castl to make it suitable for a scary witch?

## IDEA!

The Goo Grower and the Goo Shrinker can add a fun twist to your Toy Box play.

## IDEA!

The ESPN Bowling Ball can be used with destructible blocks for a giant bowling game.

Why not set up an epic paintball battle between Captain Jack Sparrow and Wreck-It Ralph, or build a jungle filled with wild animals for Mr. Incredible to battle through?